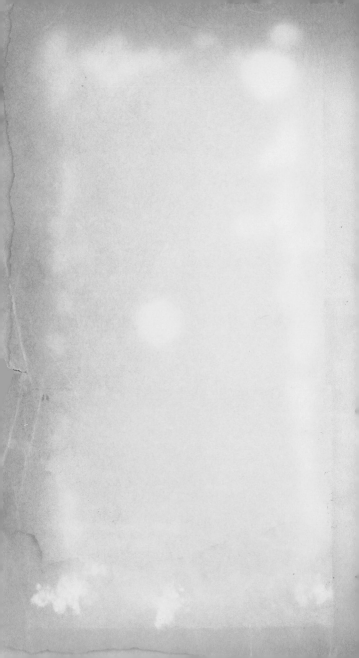

ALL THIS
AND SNOOPY,
TOO

ALL THIS AND SNOOPY, TOO

Selected Cartoons from
YOU CANT WIN, CHARLIE BROWN
VOL 1

By CHARLES M. SCHULZ

FAWCETT CREST • NEW YORK

A Fawcett Crest Book

Published by Ballantine Books

Contents of Book: PEANUTS® comic strips by Charles M. Schulz
Copyright © 1960, 1961, 1962 by United Feature Syndicate.

 Published in the United States by Ballantine Books, a division of Random House, Inc., New York, and simultaneously in Canada by Random House of Canada Limited, Toronto.

ISBN 0-449-20434-0

This book comprises the first half of YOU CAN'T WIN, CHARLIE BROWN, and is reprinted by arrangement with Holt, Rinehart and Winston.

Manufactured in the United States of America

First Fawcett Crest Edition: February 1969
First Ballantine Books Edition: April 1983

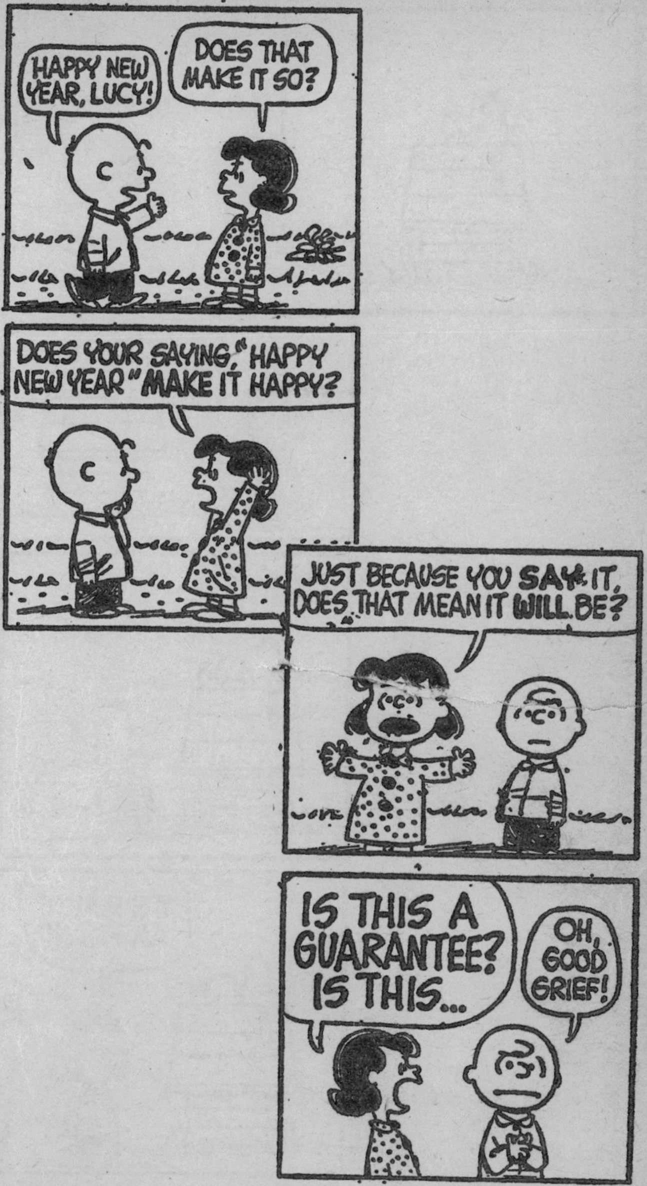
HAPPY NEW YEAR, LUCY!
DOES THAT MAKE IT SO?
DOES YOUR SAYING, "HAPPY NEW YEAR" MAKE IT HAPPY?
JUST BECAUSE YOU SAY IT, DOES THAT MEAN IT WILL BE?
IS THIS A GUARANTEE? IS THIS...
OH, GOOD GRIEF!

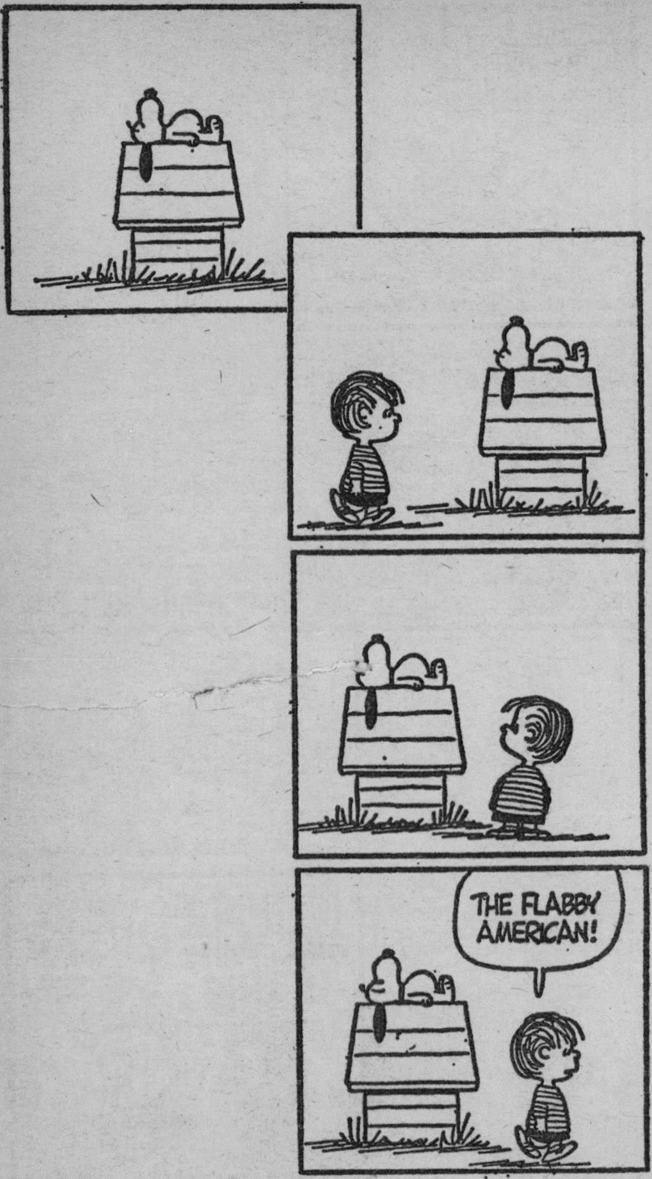
THE FLABBY AMERICAN!

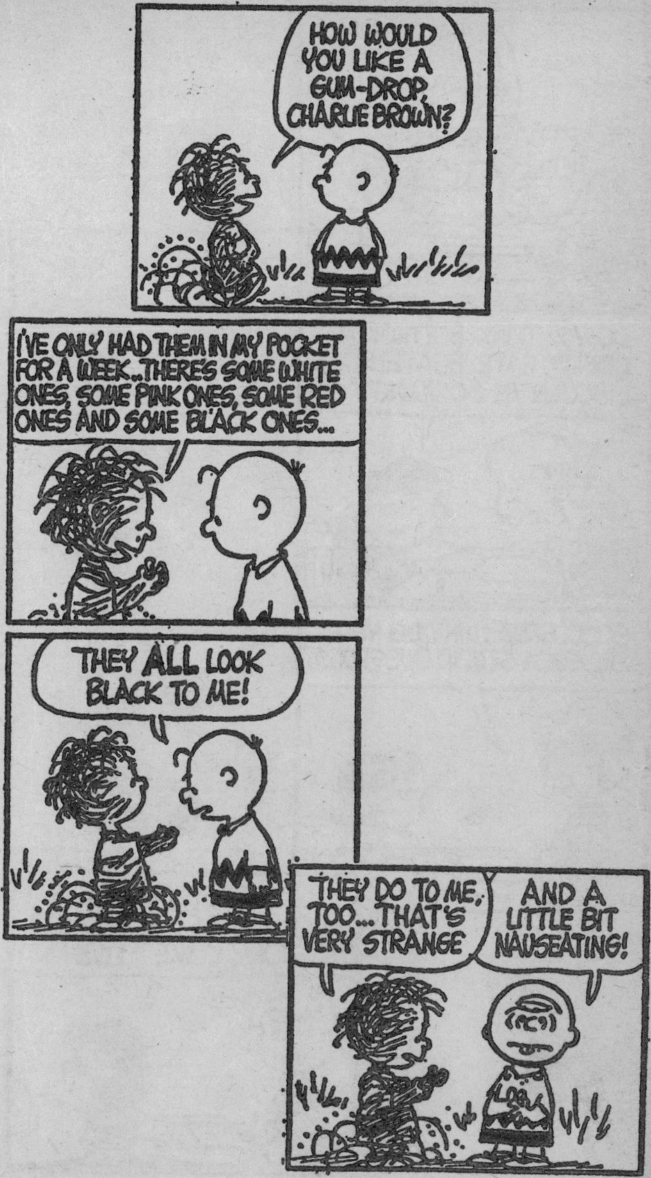
HOW WOULD YOU LIKE A GUM-DROP, CHARLIE BROWN?
I'VE ONLY HAD THEM IN MY POCKET FOR A WEEK..THERE'S SOME WHITE ONES, SOME PINK ONES, SOME RED ONES AND SOME BLACK ONES...
THEY ALL LOOK BLACK TO ME!
THEY DO TO ME, TOO...THAT'S VERY STRANGE
AND A LITTLE BIT NAUSEATING!

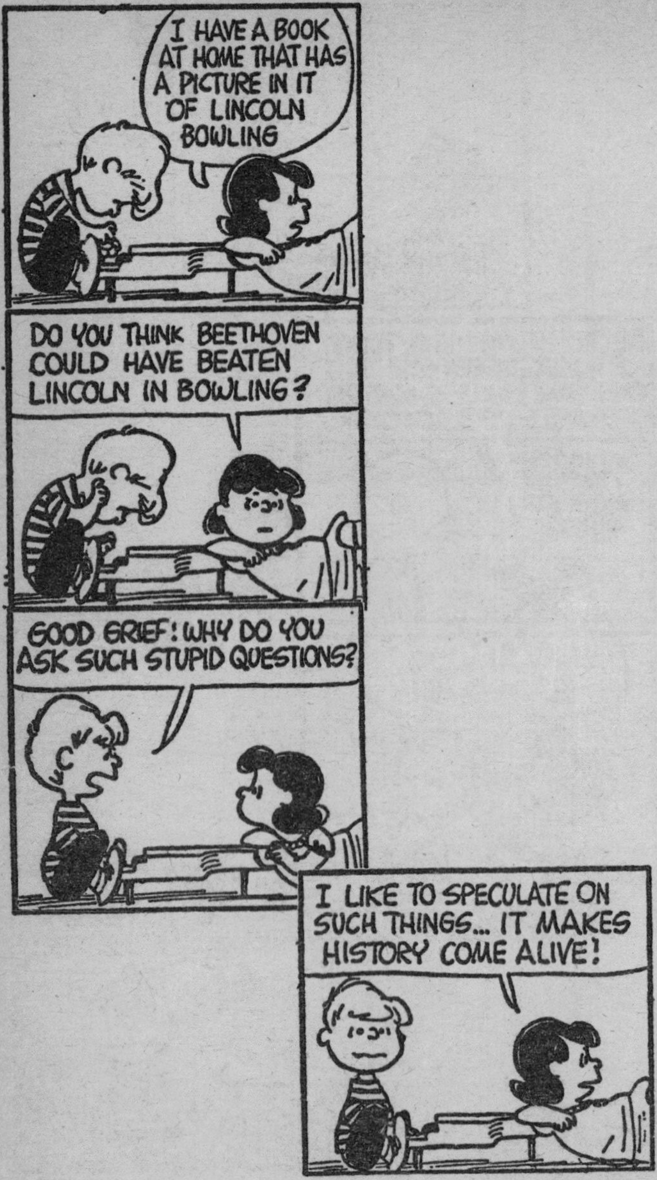
I HAVE A BOOK AT HOME THAT HAS A PICTURE IN IT OF LINCOLN BOWLING
DO YOU THINK BEETHOVEN COULD HAVE BEATEN LINCOLN IN BOWLING?
GOOD GRIEF! WHY DO YOU ASK SUCH STUPID QUESTIONS?
I LIKE TO SPECULATE ON SUCH THINGS... IT MAKES HISTORY COME ALIVE!

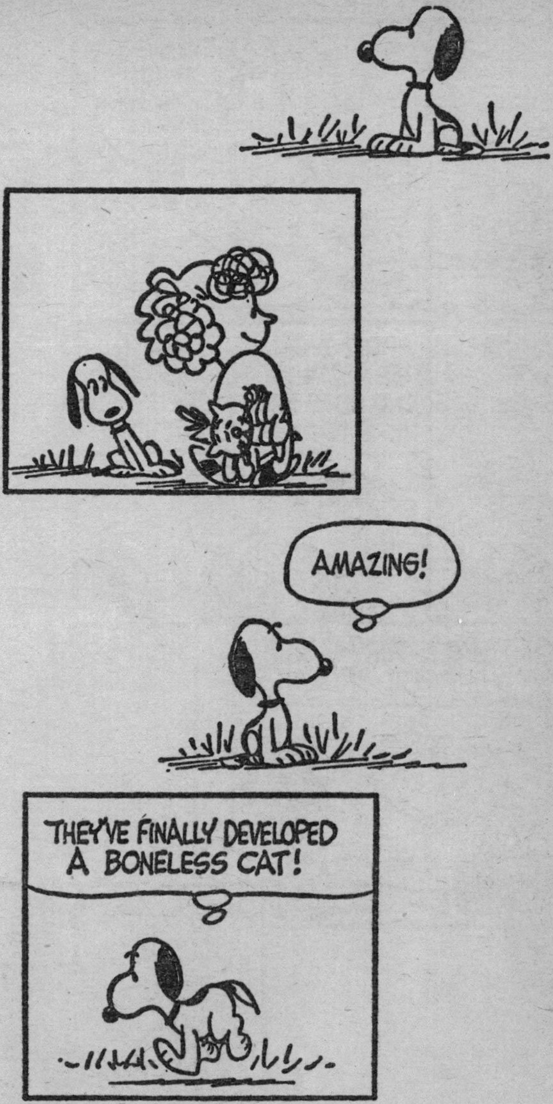
AMAZING!
THEY'VE FINALLY DEVELOPED A BONELESS CAT!

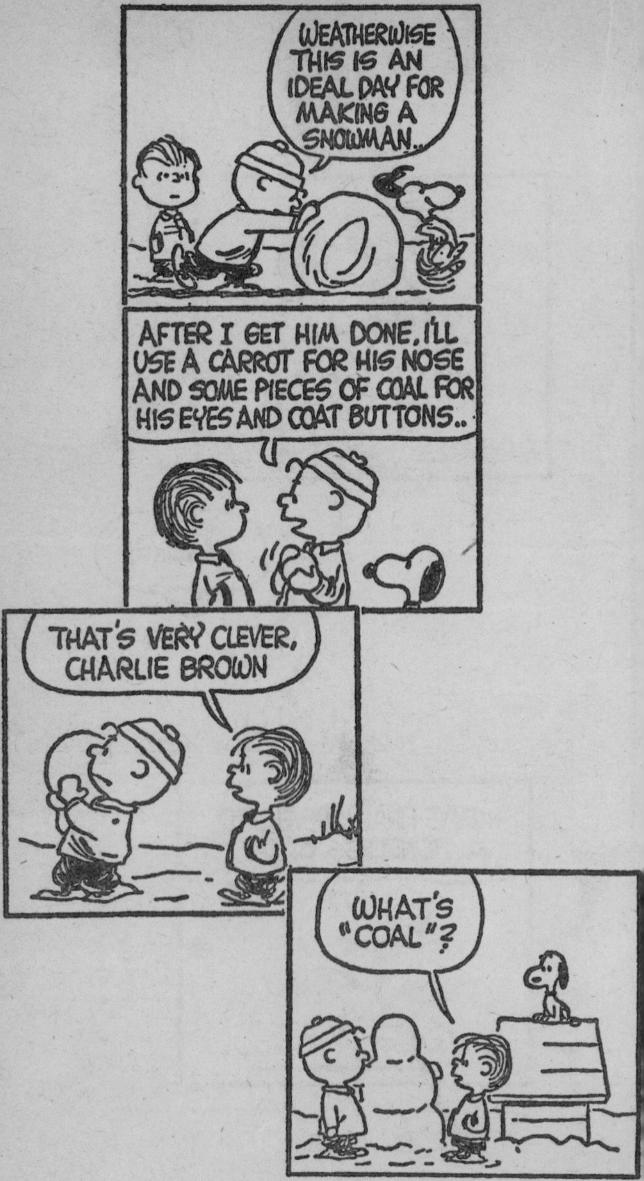
WEATHERWISE THIS IS AN IDEAL DAY FOR MAKING A SNOWMAN..
AFTER I GET HIM DONE, I'LL USE A CARROT FOR HIS NOSE AND SOME PIECES OF COAL FOR HIS EYES AND COAT BUTTONS..
THAT'S VERY CLEVER, CHARLIE BROWN
WHAT'S "COAL"?

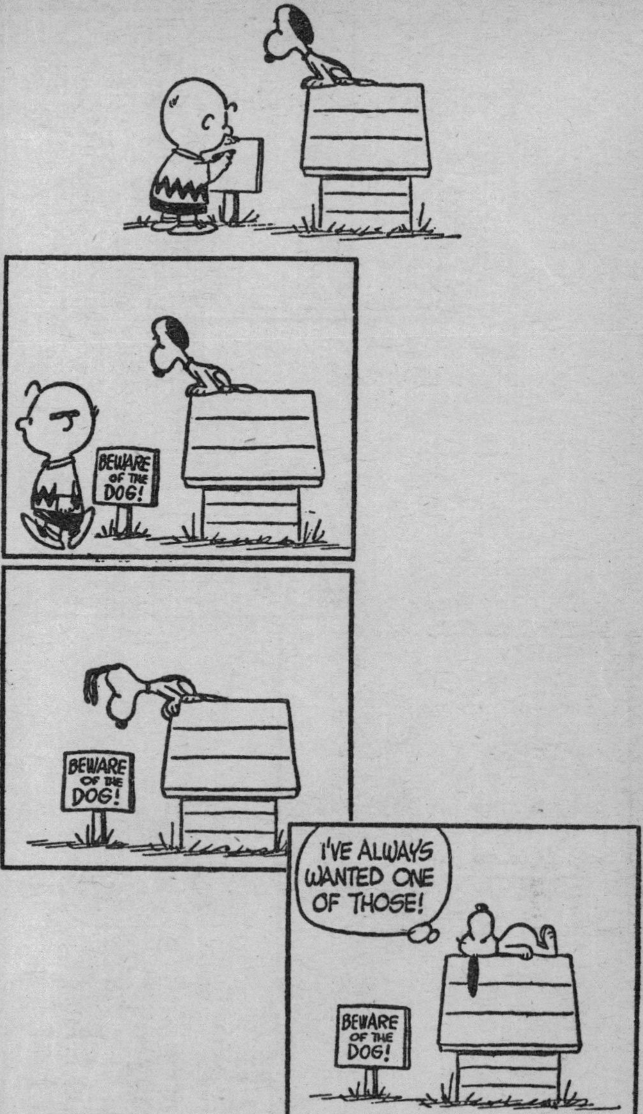
BEWARE OF THE DOG!
BEWARE OF THE DOG!
I'VE ALWAYS WANTED ONE OF THOSE!
BEWARE OF THE DOG!

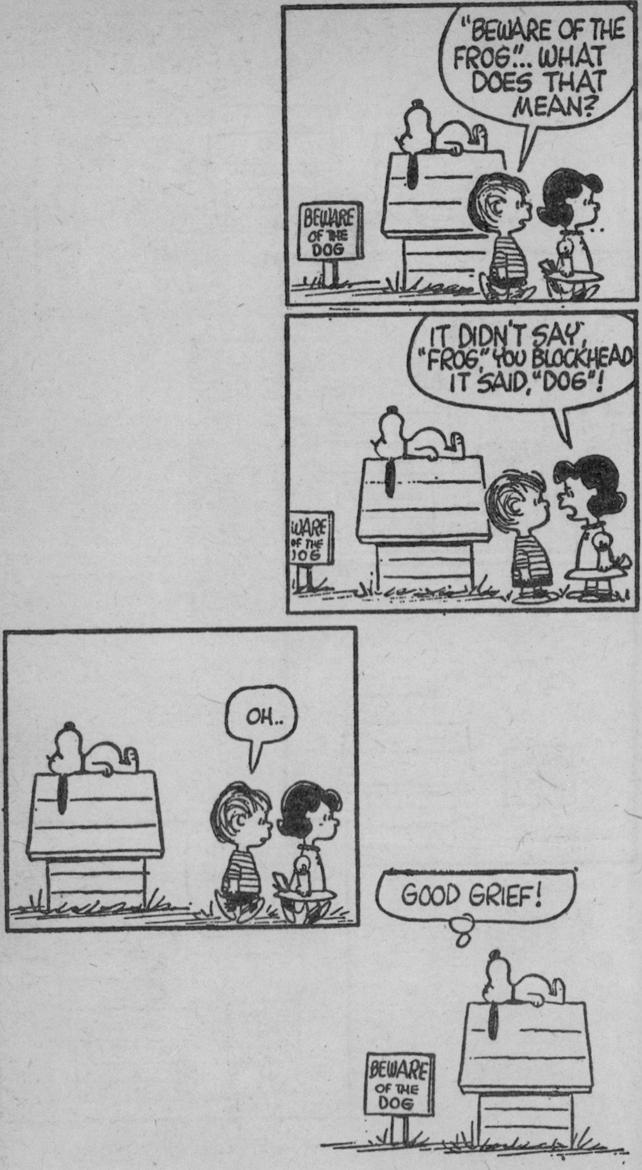
"BEWARE OF THE FROG"... WHAT DOES THAT MEAN?
BEWARE OF THE DOG
IT DIDN'T SAY, "FROG," YOU BLOCKHEAD IT SAID, "DOG"!
OH..
GOOD GRIEF!
BEWARE OF THE DOG

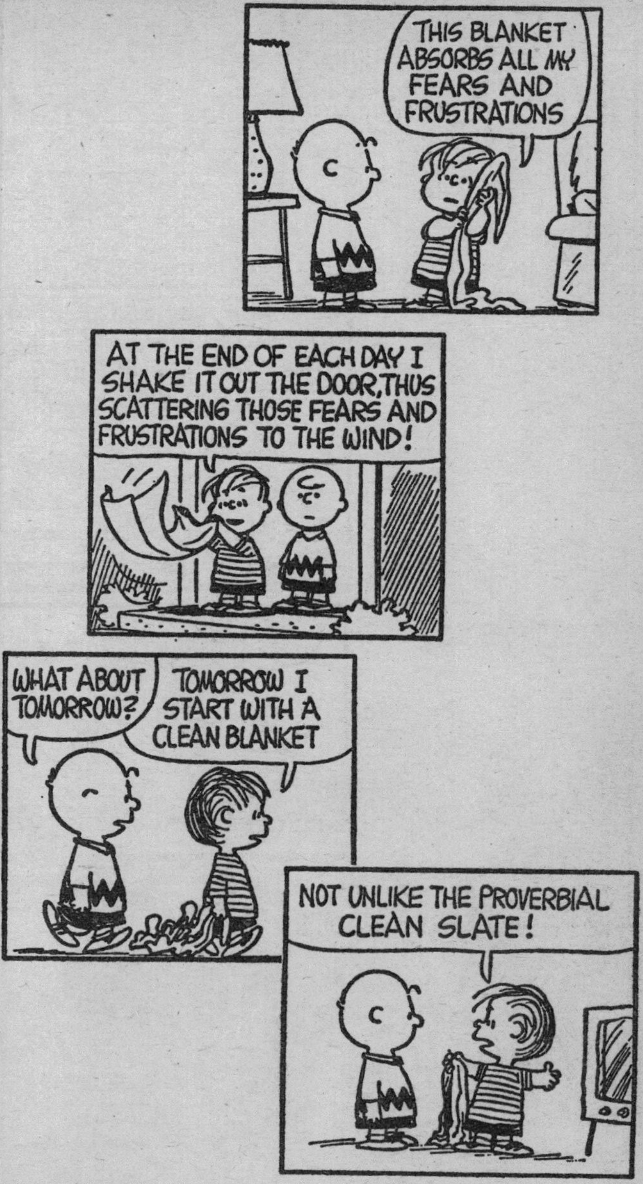
THIS BLANKET ABSORBS ALL MY FEARS AND FRUSTRATIONS
AT THE END OF EACH DAY I SHAKE IT OUT THE DOOR, THUS SCATTERING THOSE FEARS AND FRUSTRATIONS TO THE WIND!
WHAT ABOUT TOMORROW?
TOMORROW I START WITH A CLEAN BLANKET
NOT UNLIKE THE PROVERBIAL CLEAN SLATE!

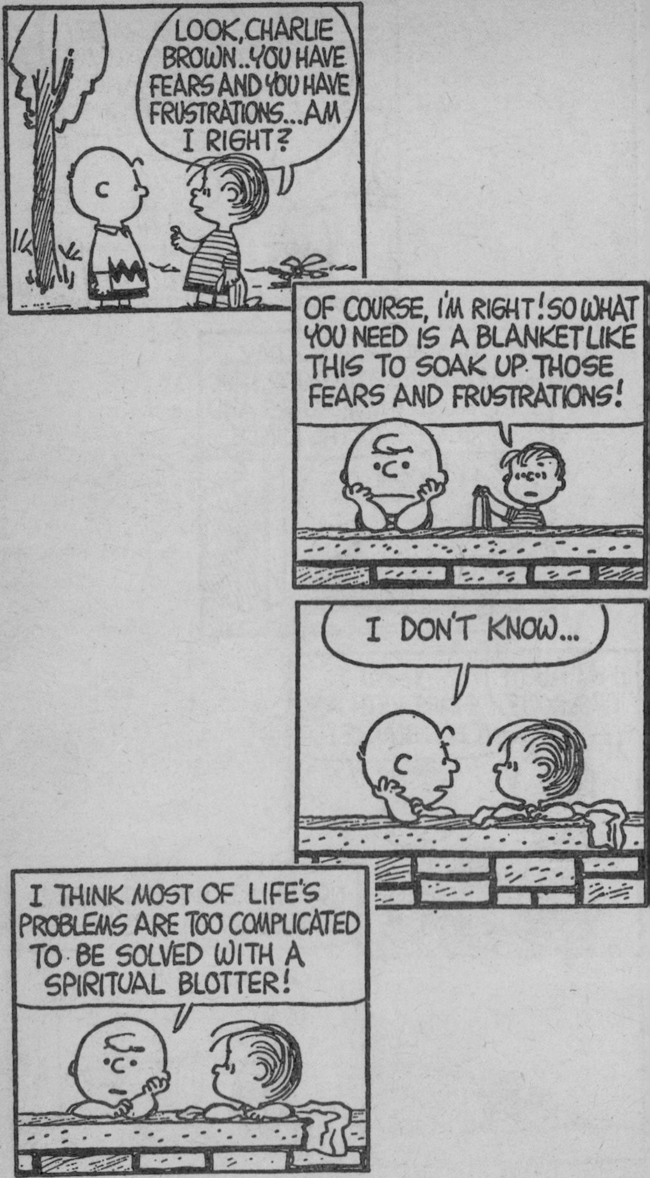
LOOK, CHARLIE BROWN..YOU HAVE FEARS AND YOU HAVE FRUSTRATIONS...AM I RIGHT?
OF COURSE, I'M RIGHT! SO WHAT YOU NEED IS A BLANKET LIKE THIS TO SOAK UP THOSE FEARS AND FRUSTRATIONS!
I DON'T KNOW...
I THINK MOST OF LIFE'S PROBLEMS ARE TOO COMPLICATED TO BE SOLVED WITH A SPIRITUAL BLOTTER!

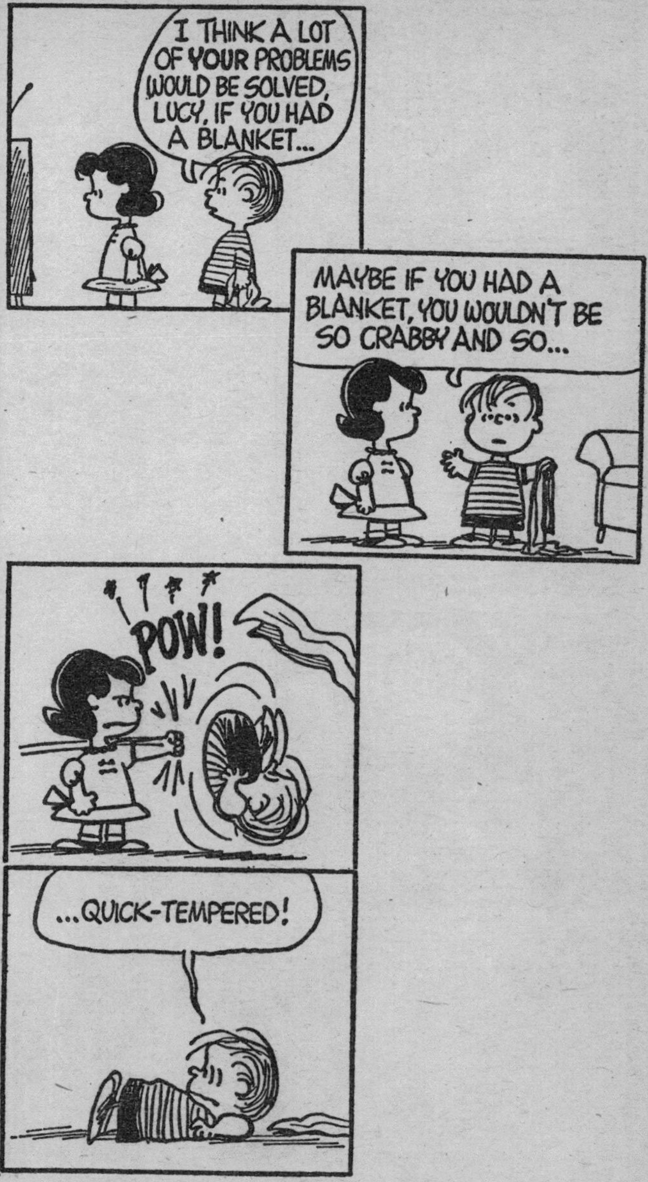
I THINK A LOT OF YOUR PROBLEMS WOULD BE SOLVED, LUCY, IF YOU HAD A BLANKET...
MAYBE IF YOU HAD A BLANKET, YOU WOULDN'T BE SO CRABBY AND SO...
POW!
...QUICK-TEMPERED!

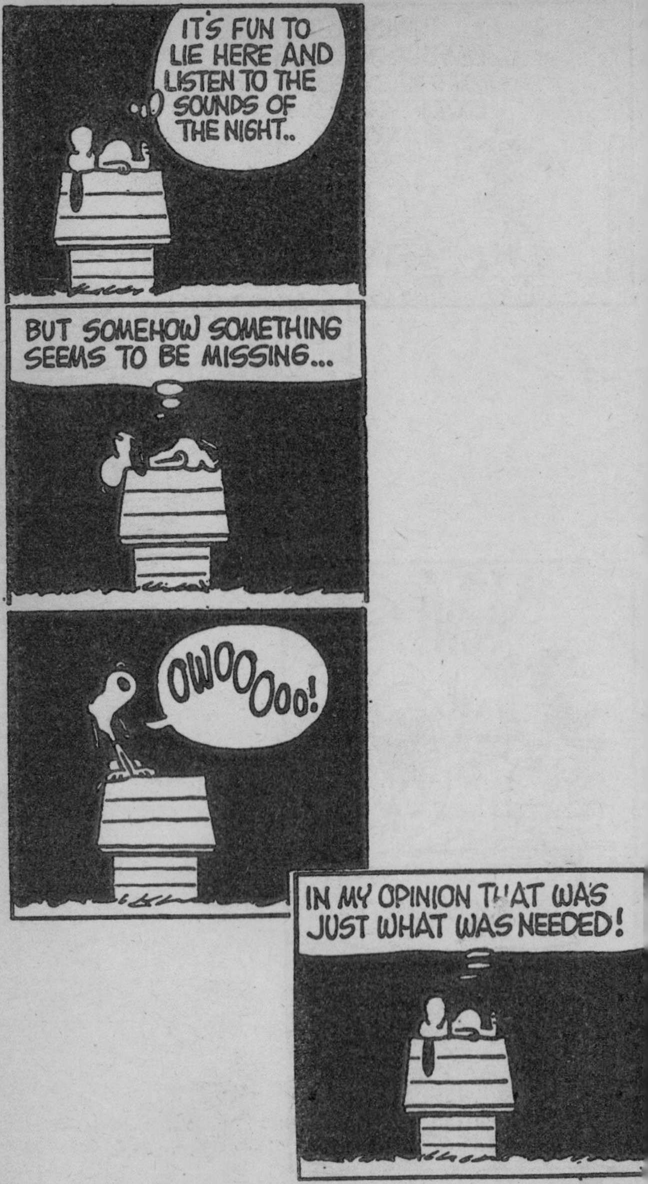
IT'S FUN TO LIE HERE AND LISTEN TO THE SOUNDS OF THE NIGHT..
BUT SOMEHOW SOMETHING SEEMS TO BE MISSING...
OWOOOOoo!
IN MY OPINION THAT WAS JUST WHAT WAS NEEDED!

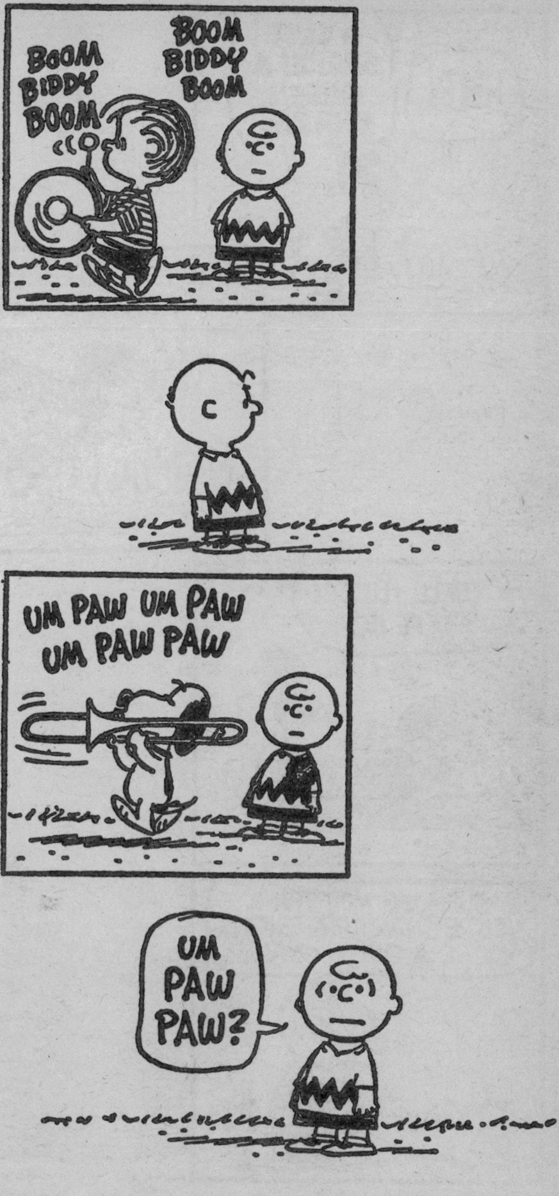
BOOM BIDDY BOOM
BOOM BIDDY BOOM
UM PAW UM PAW UM PAW PAW
UM PAW PAW?

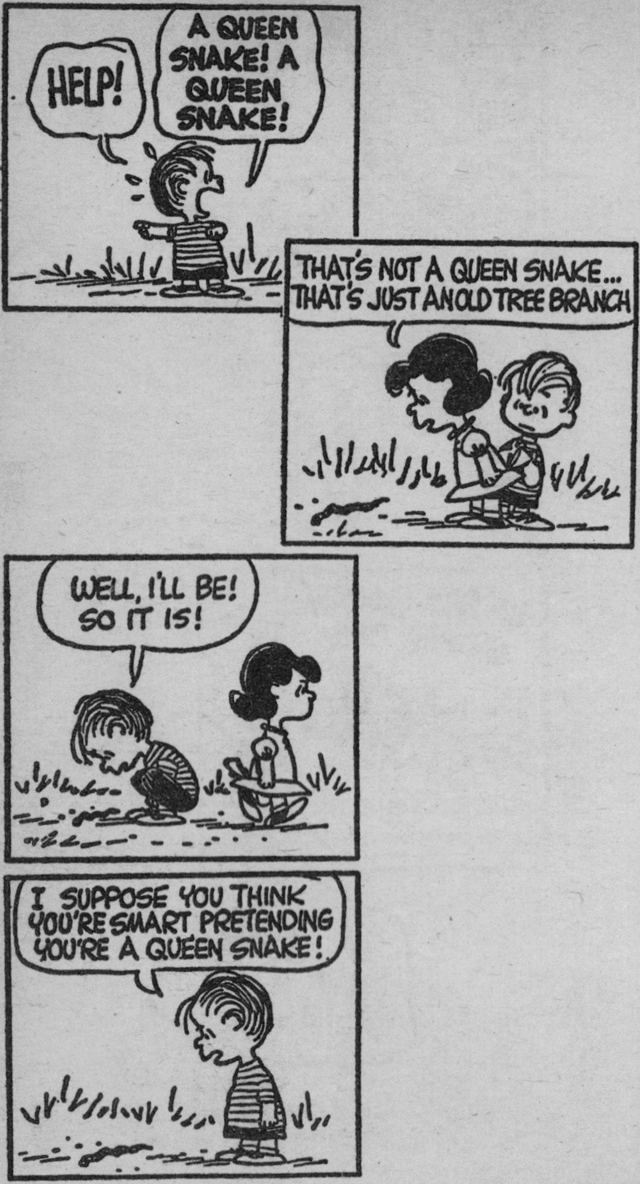
HELP!
A QUEEN SNAKE! A QUEEN SNAKE!
THAT'S NOT A QUEEN SNAKE... THAT'S JUST AN OLD TREE BRANCH
WELL, I'LL BE! SO IT IS!
I SUPPOSE YOU THINK YOU'RE SMART PRETENDING YOU'RE A QUEEN SNAKE!

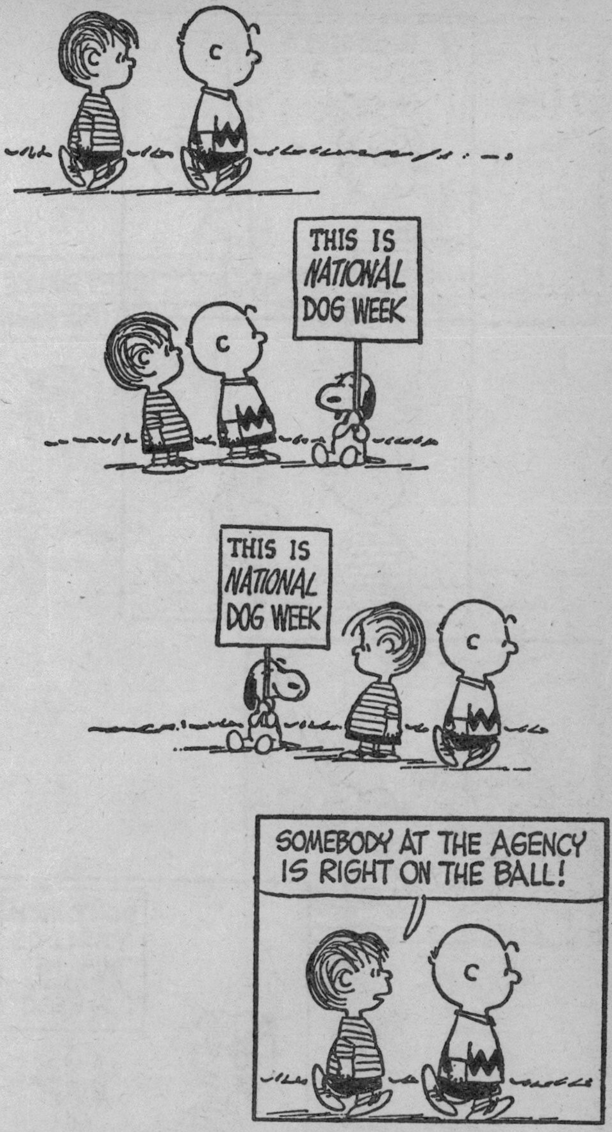
THIS IS NATIONAL DOG WEEK
THIS IS NATIONAL DOG WEEK
SOMEBODY AT THE AGENCY IS RIGHT ON THE BALL!

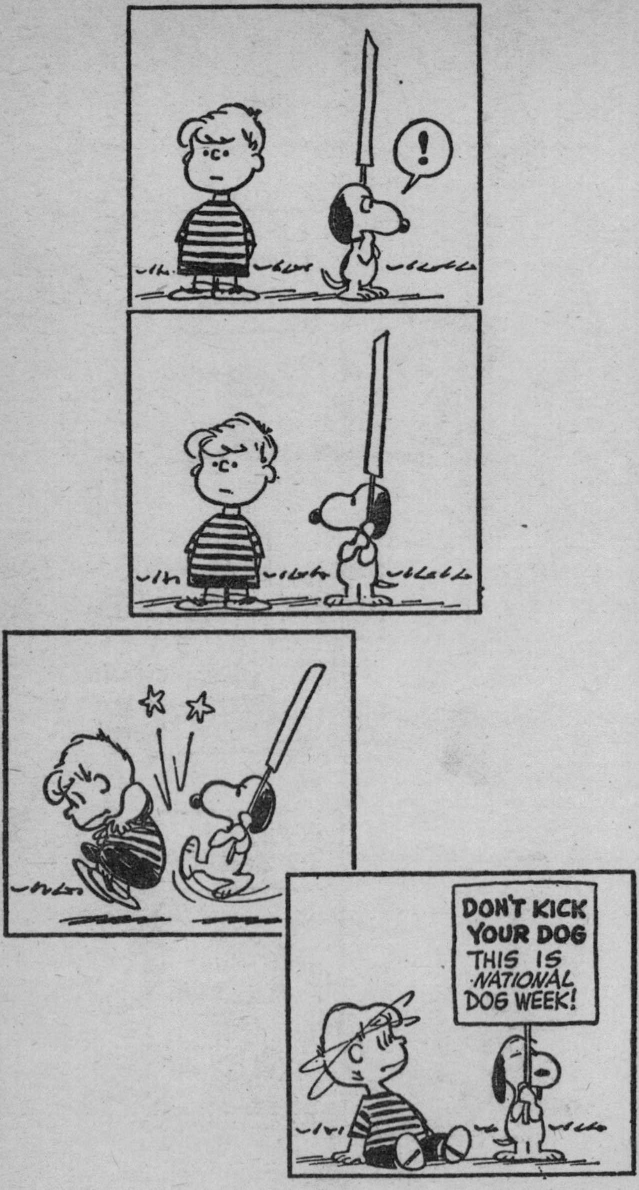
!
DON'T KICK YOUR DOG
THIS IS NATIONAL DOG WEEK!

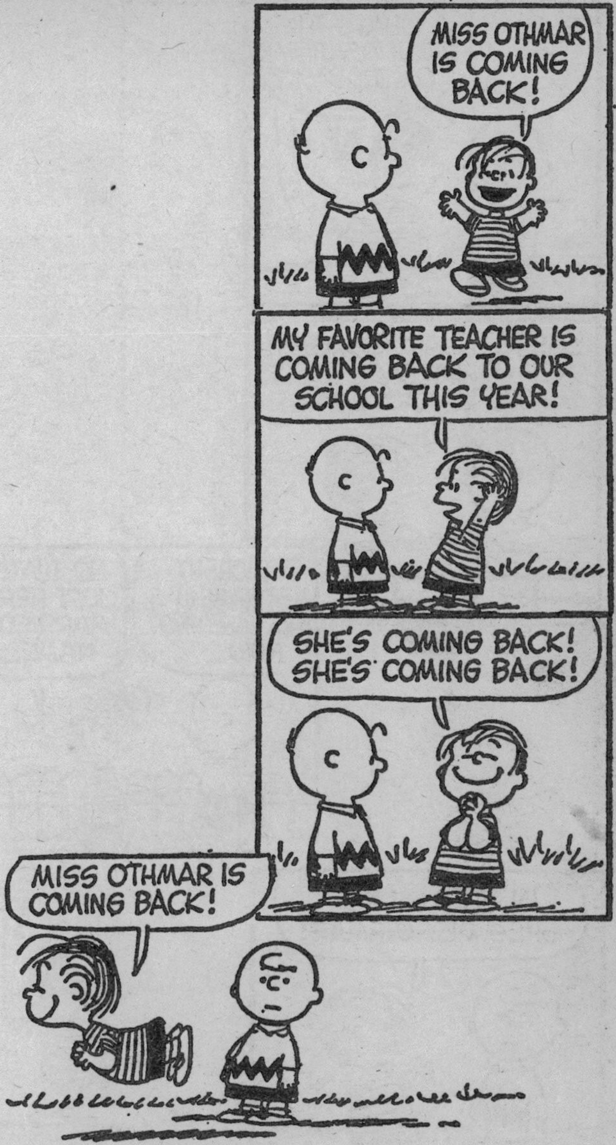
MISS OTHMAR IS COMING BACK!
MY FAVORITE TEACHER IS COMING BACK TO OUR SCHOOL THIS YEAR!
SHE'S COMING BACK! SHE'S COMING BACK!
MISS OTHMAR IS COMING BACK!

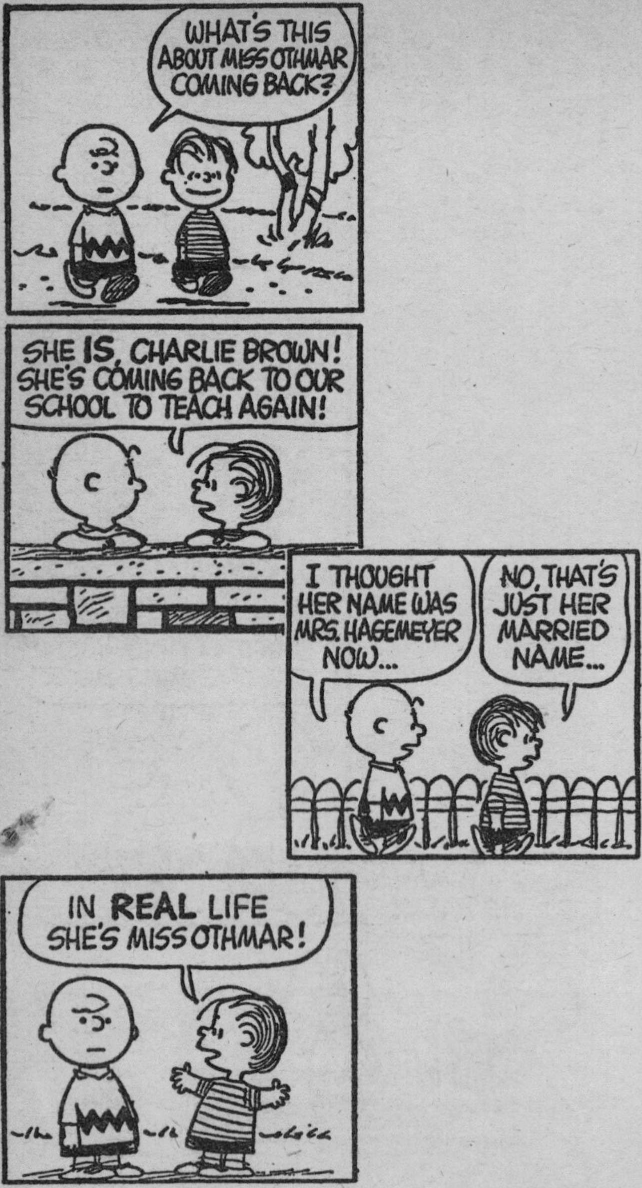
WHAT'S THIS ABOUT MISS OTHMAR COMING BACK?
SHE IS, CHARLIE BROWN! SHE'S COMING BACK TO OUR SCHOOL TO TEACH AGAIN!
I THOUGHT HER NAME WAS MRS. HAGEMEYER NOW...
NO, THAT'S JUST HER MARRIED NAME...
IN REAL LIFE SHE'S MISS OTHMAR!

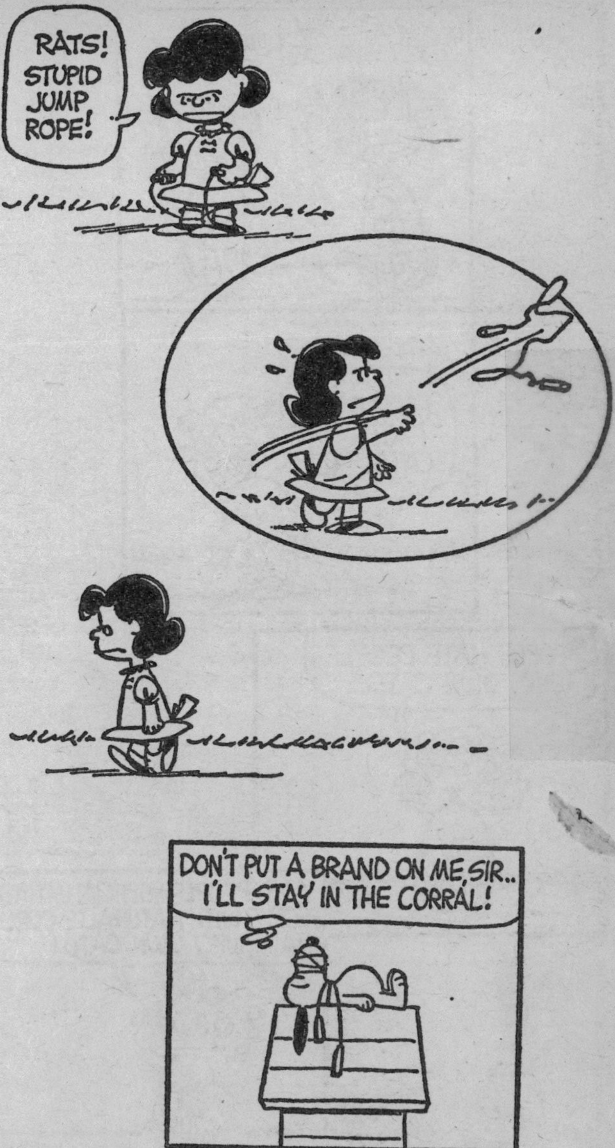
RATS! STUPID JUMP ROPE!
DON'T PUT A BRAND ON ME, SIR.. I'LL STAY IN THE CORRAL!

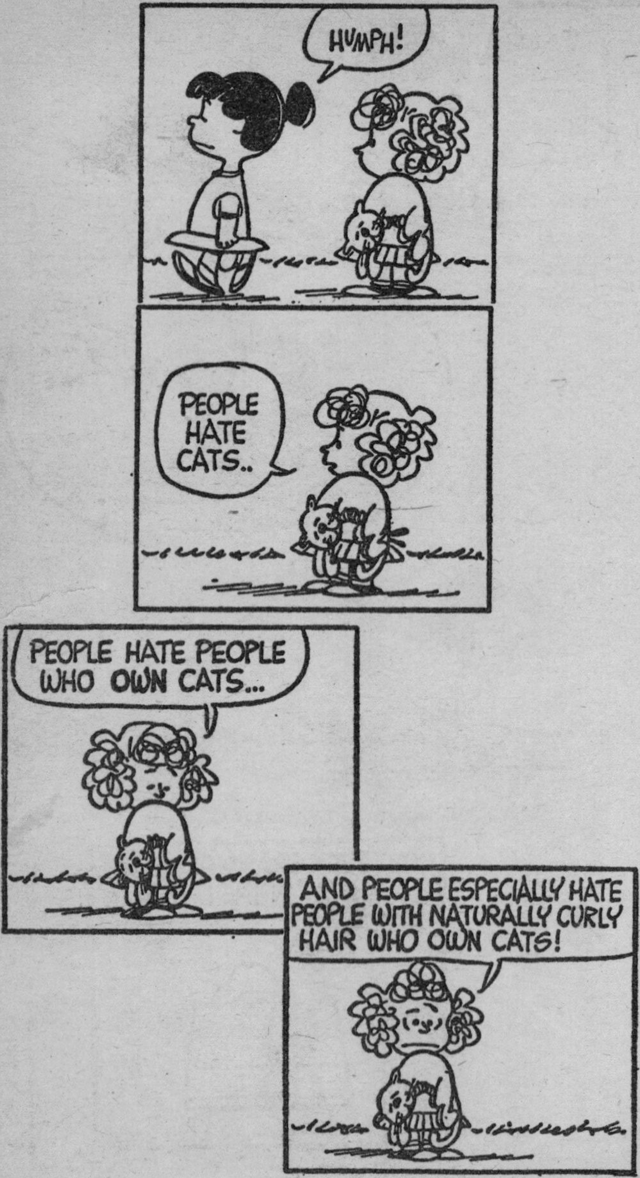
HUMPH!
PEOPLE HATE CATS..
PEOPLE HATE PEOPLE WHO OWN CATS...
AND PEOPLE ESPECIALLY HATE PEOPLE WITH NATURALLY CURLY HAIR WHO OWN CATS!

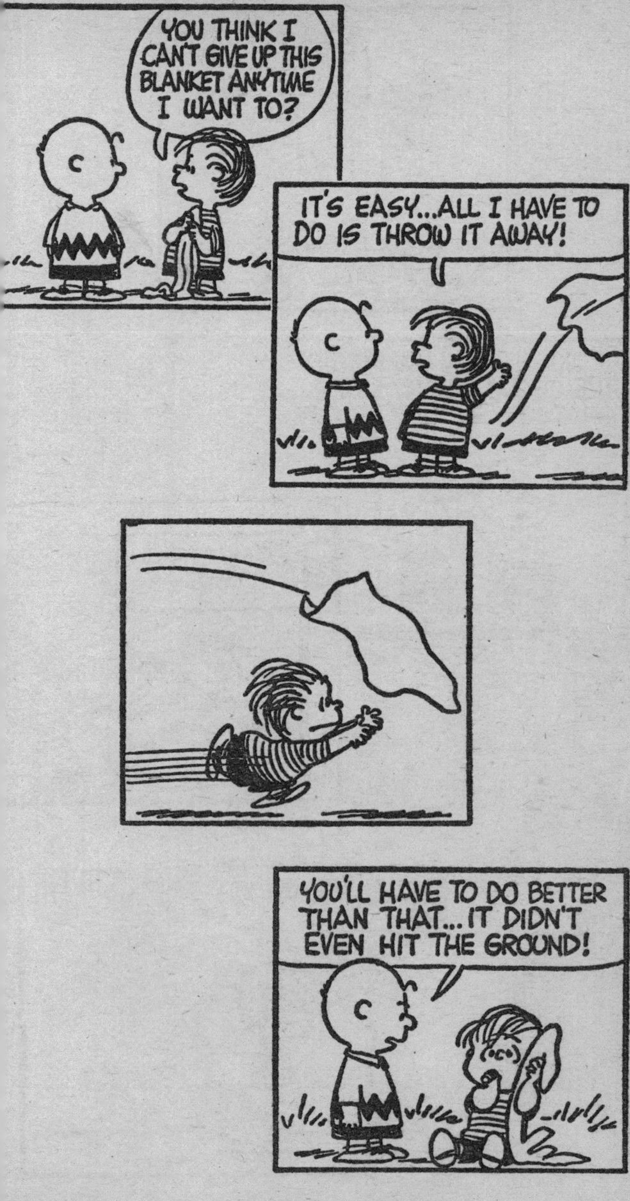
YOU THINK I CAN'T GIVE UP THIS BLANKET ANYTIME I WANT TO?
IT'S EASY...ALL I HAVE TO DO IS THROW IT AWAY!
YOU'LL HAVE TO DO BETTER THAN THAT...IT DIDN'T EVEN HIT THE GROUND!

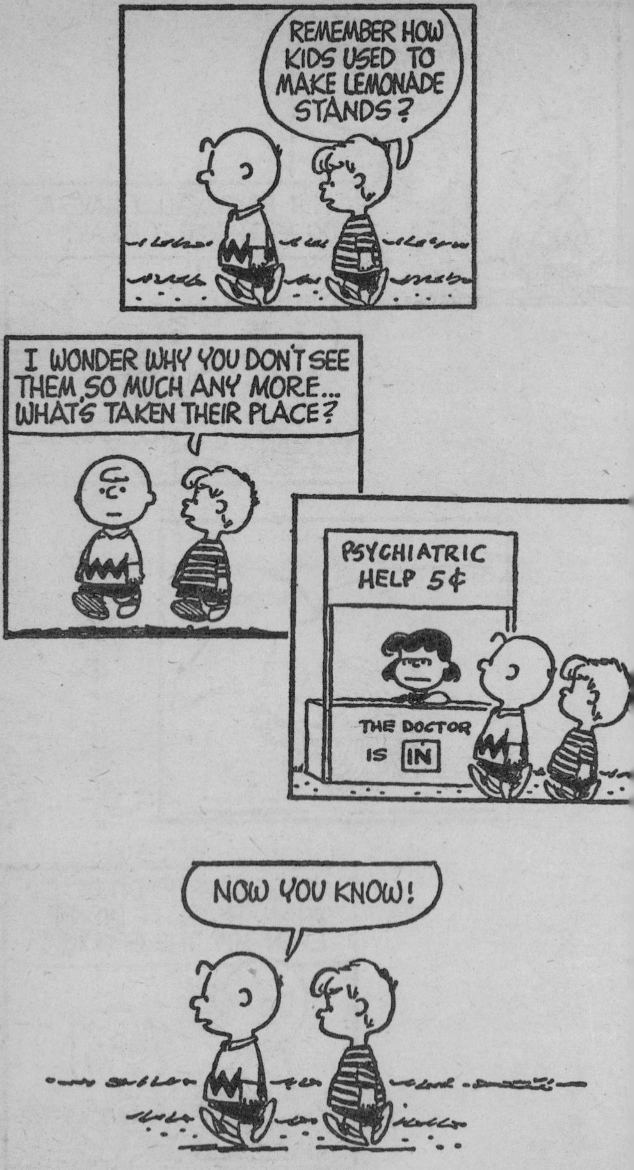
REMEMBER HOW KIDS USED TO MAKE LEMONADE STANDS?
I WONDER WHY YOU DON'T SEE THEM SO MUCH ANY MORE... WHAT'S TAKEN THEIR PLACE?
PSYCHIATRIC HELP 5¢
THE DOCTOR IS IN
NOW YOU KNOW!

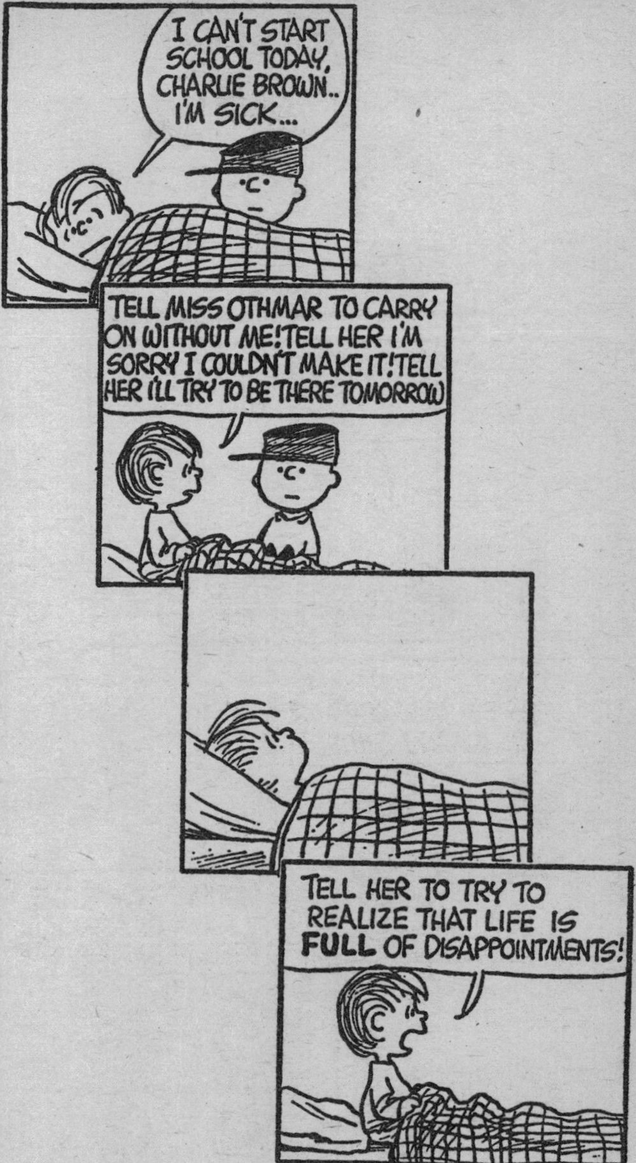
I CAN'T START SCHOOL TODAY, CHARLIE BROWN.. I'M SICK...
TELL MISS OTHMAR TO CARRY ON WITHOUT ME! TELL HER I'M SORRY I COULDN'T MAKE IT! TELL HER I'LL TRY TO BE THERE TOMORROW
TELL HER TO TRY TO REALIZE THAT LIFE IS FULL OF DISAPPOINTMENTS!

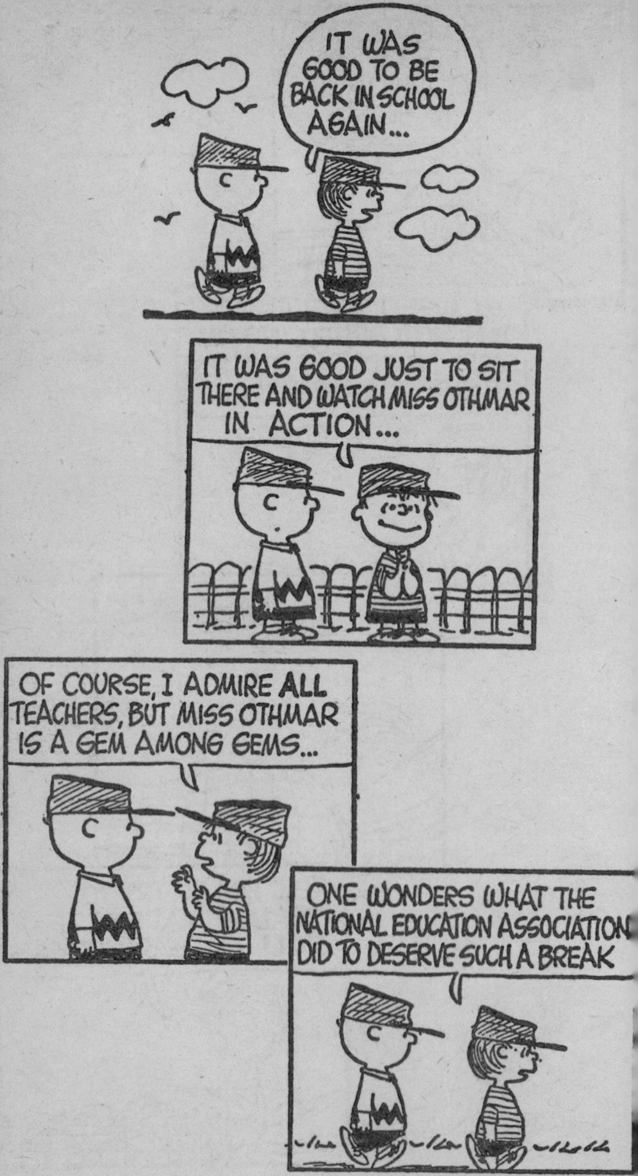
IT WAS GOOD TO BE BACK IN SCHOOL AGAIN...
IT WAS GOOD JUST TO SIT THERE AND WATCH MISS OTHMAR IN ACTION...
OF COURSE, I ADMIRE ALL TEACHERS, BUT MISS OTHMAR IS A GEM AMONG GEMS...
ONE WONDERS WHAT THE NATIONAL EDUCATION ASSOCIATION DID TO DESERVE SUCH A BREAK

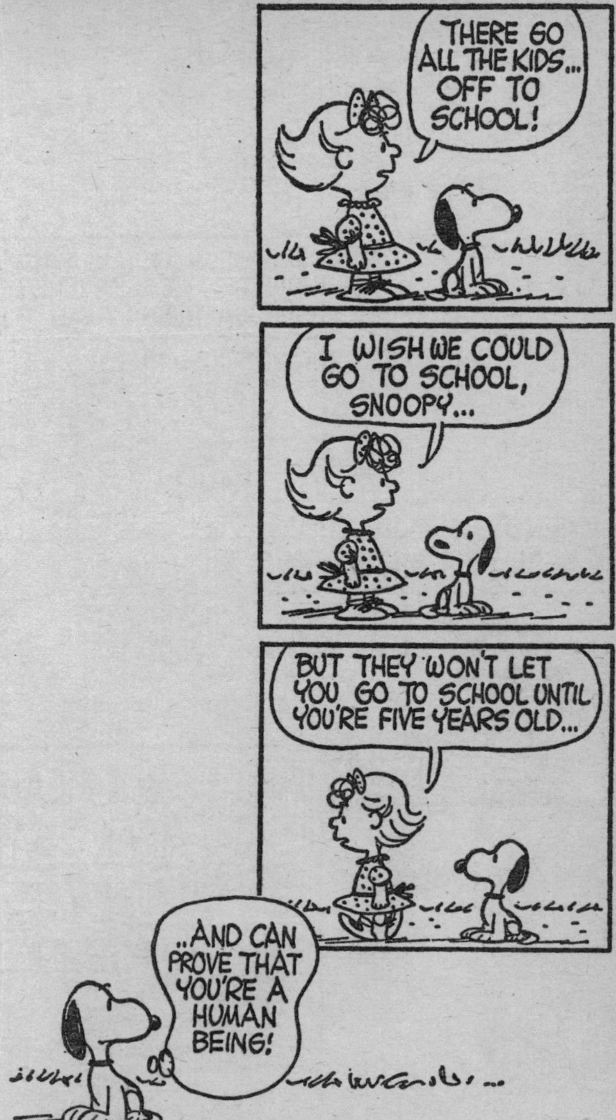
THERE GO ALL THE KIDS... OFF TO SCHOOL!
I WISH WE COULD GO TO SCHOOL, SNOOPY...
BUT THEY WON'T LET YOU GO TO SCHOOL UNTIL YOU'RE FIVE YEARS OLD...
..AND CAN PROVE THAT YOU'RE A HUMAN BEING!

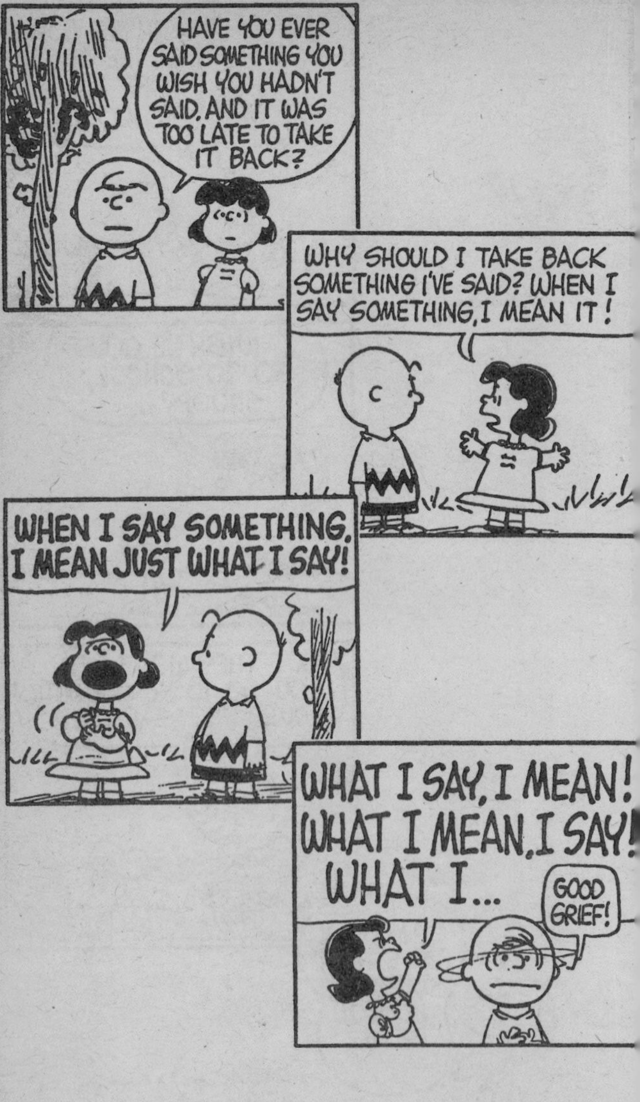
HAVE YOU EVER SAID SOMETHING YOU WISH YOU HADN'T SAID, AND IT WAS TOO LATE TO TAKE IT BACK?
WHY SHOULD I TAKE BACK SOMETHING I'VE SAID? WHEN I SAY SOMETHING, I MEAN IT!
WHEN I SAY SOMETHING, I MEAN JUST WHAT I SAY!
WHAT I SAY, I MEAN! WHAT I MEAN, I SAY! WHAT I...
GOOD GRIEF!

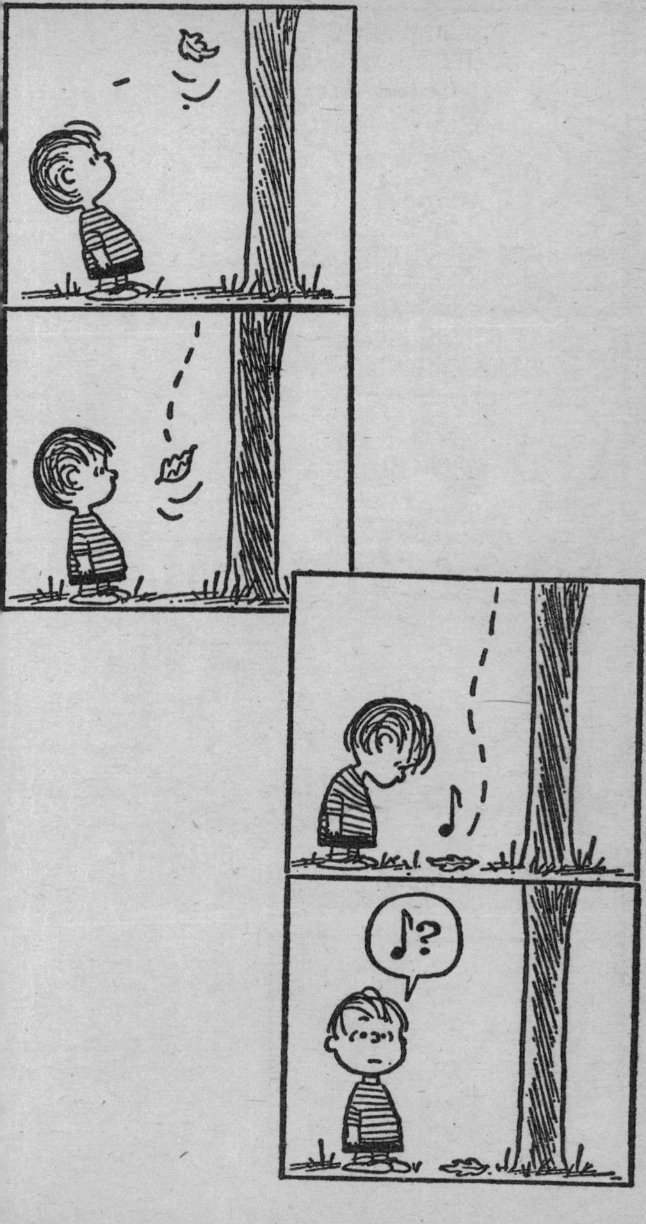
♪?

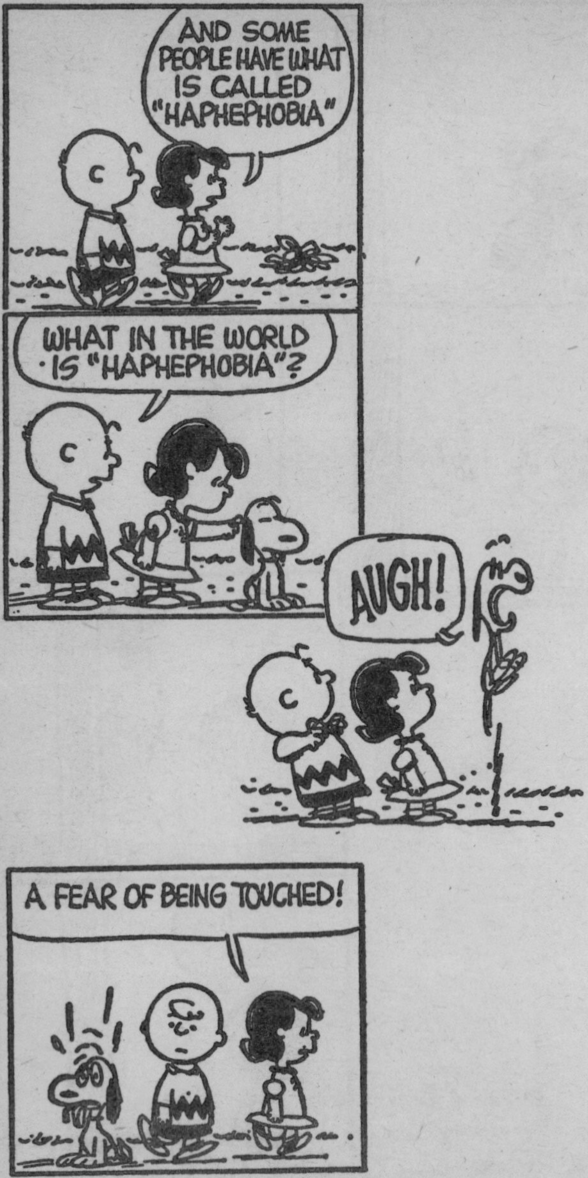
AND SOME PEOPLE HAVE WHAT IS CALLED "HAPHEPHOBIA"
WHAT IN THE WORLD IS "HAPHEPHOBIA"?
AUGH!
A FEAR OF BEING TOUCHED!

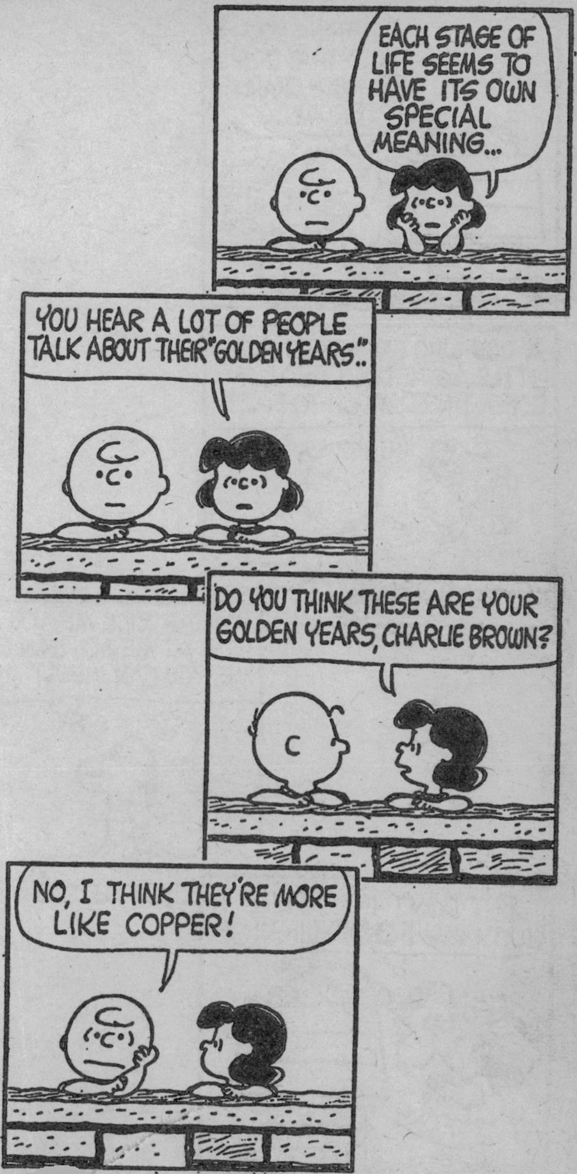
EACH STAGE OF LIFE SEEMS TO HAVE ITS OWN SPECIAL MEANING...
YOU HEAR A LOT OF PEOPLE TALK ABOUT THEIR "GOLDEN YEARS."..
DO YOU THINK THESE ARE YOUR GOLDEN YEARS, CHARLIE BROWN?
NO, I THINK THEY'RE MORE LIKE COPPER!

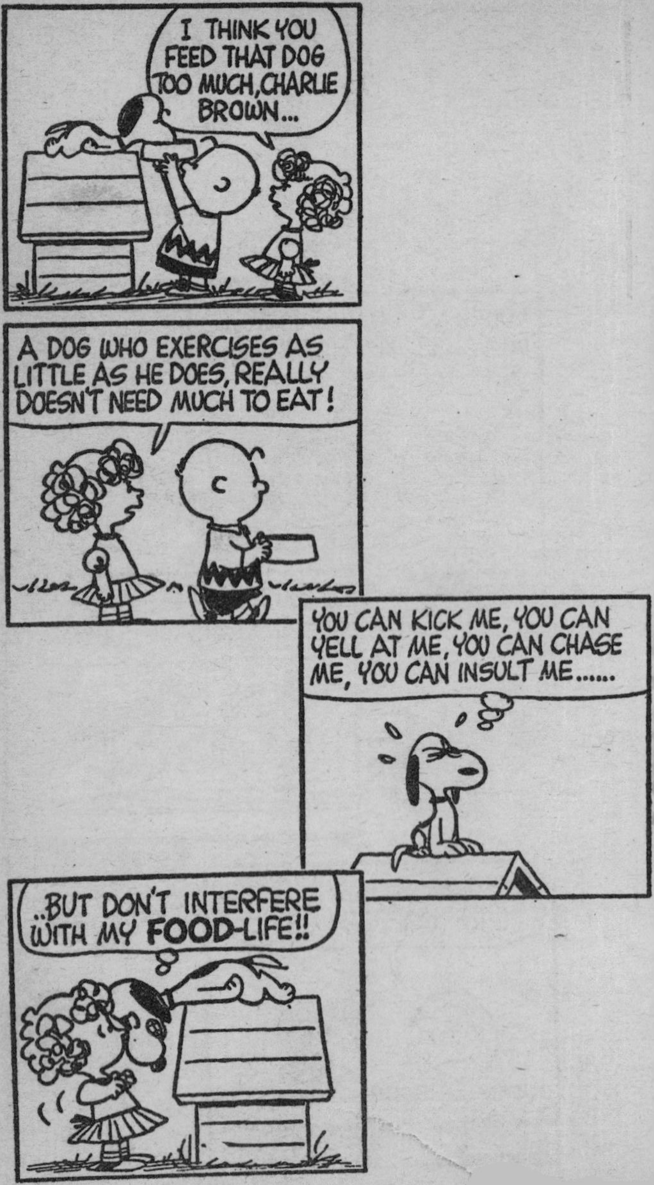
I THINK YOU FEED THAT DOG TOO MUCH, CHARLIE BROWN...
A DOG WHO EXERCISES AS LITTLE AS HE DOES, REALLY DOESN'T NEED MUCH TO EAT!
YOU CAN KICK ME, YOU CAN YELL AT ME, YOU CAN CHASE ME, YOU CAN INSULT ME......
..BUT DON'T INTERFERE WITH MY **FOOD**-LIFE!!

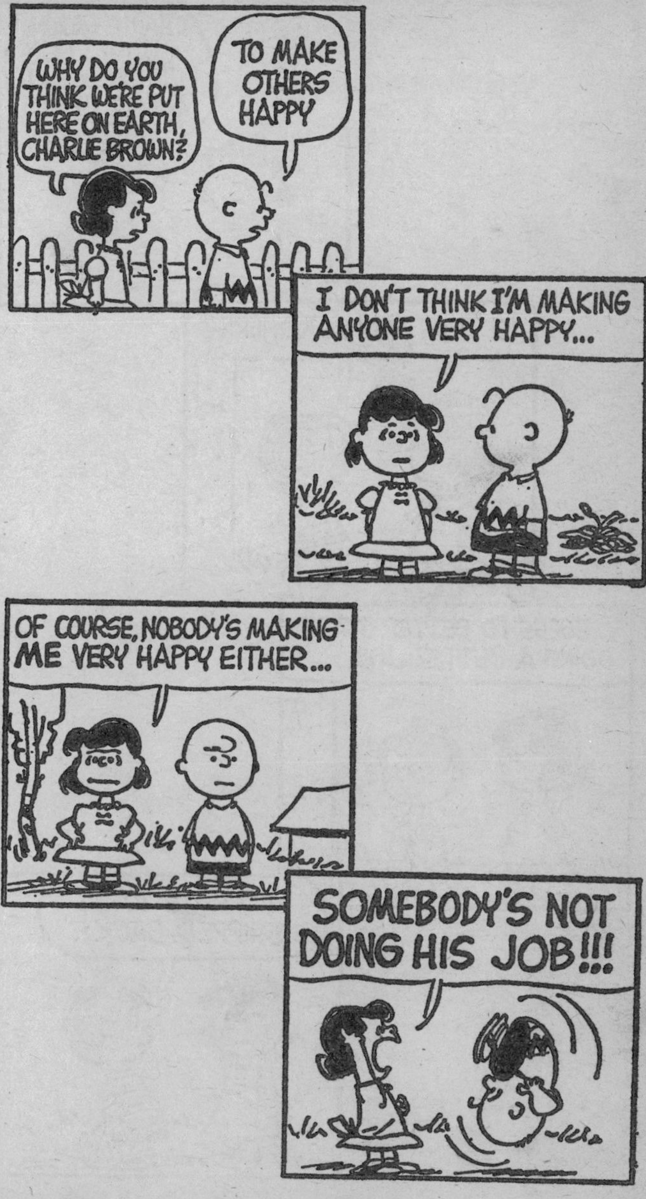
WHY DO YOU THINK WE'RE PUT HERE ON EARTH, CHARLIE BROWN?
TO MAKE OTHERS HAPPY
I DON'T THINK I'M MAKING ANYONE VERY HAPPY...
OF COURSE, NOBODY'S MAKING ME VERY HAPPY EITHER...
SOMEBODY'S NOT DOING HIS JOB!!!

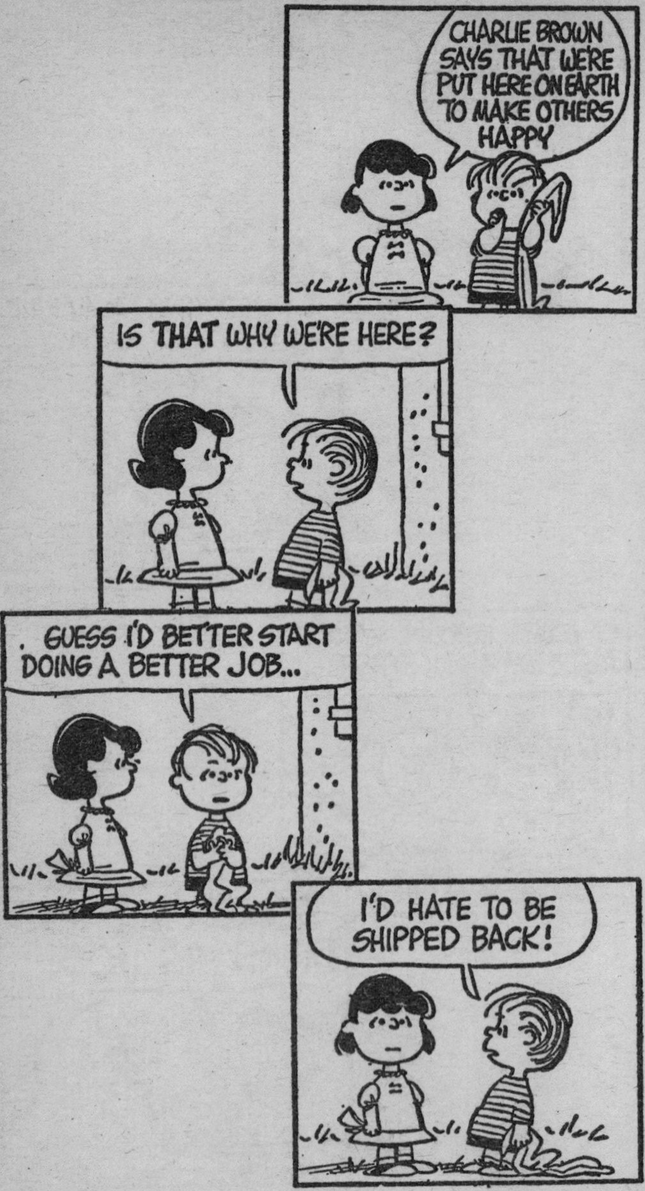
CHARLIE BROWN SAYS THAT WE'RE PUT HERE ON EARTH TO MAKE OTHERS HAPPY
IS THAT WHY WE'RE HERE?
GUESS I'D BETTER START DOING A BETTER JOB...
I'D HATE TO BE SHIPPED BACK!

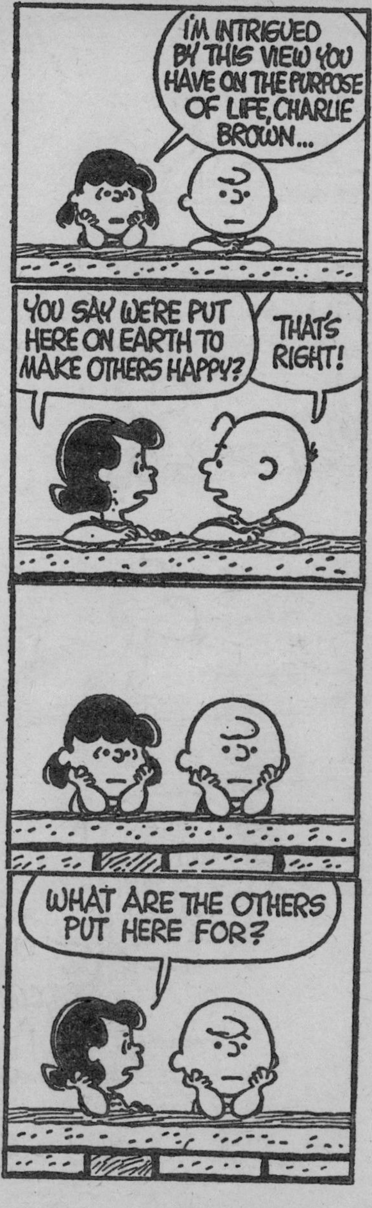
I'M INTRIGUED BY THIS VIEW YOU HAVE ON THE PURPOSE OF LIFE, CHARLIE BROWN...
YOU SAY WE'RE PUT HERE ON EARTH TO MAKE OTHERS HAPPY?
THAT'S RIGHT!
WHAT ARE THE OTHERS PUT HERE FOR?

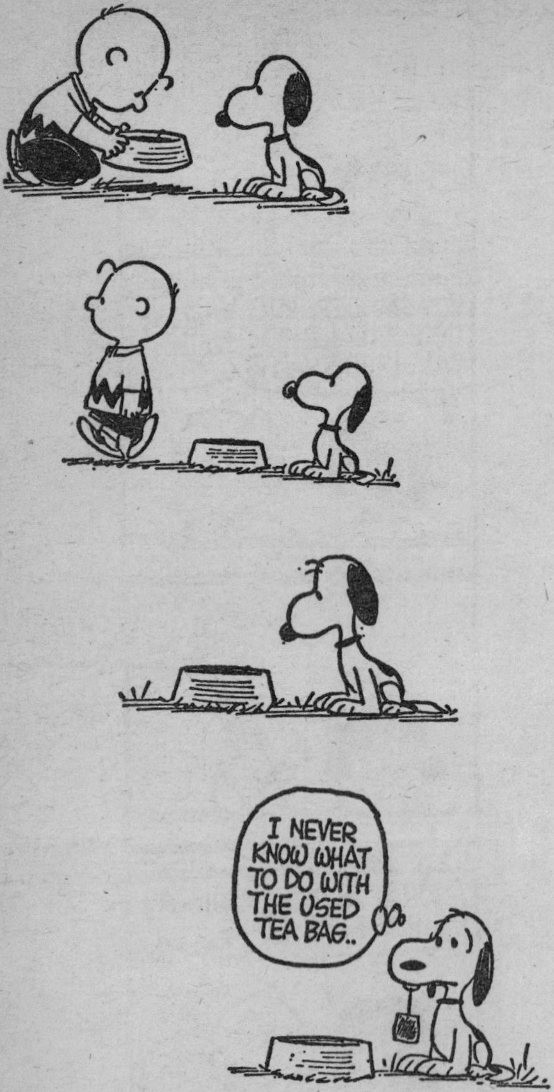
I NEVER KNOW WHAT TO DO WITH THE USED TEA BAG..

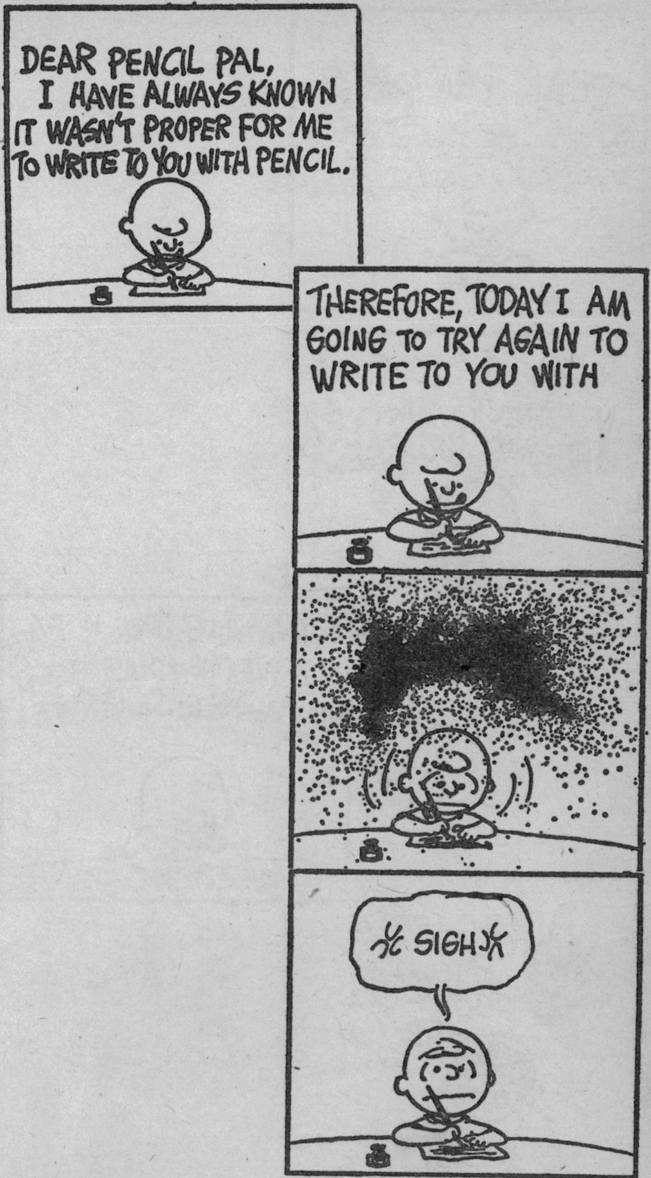
DEAR PENCIL PAL,
I HAVE ALWAYS KNOWN IT WASN'T PROPER FOR ME TO WRITE TO YOU WITH PENCIL.
THEREFORE, TODAY I AM GOING TO TRY AGAIN TO WRITE TO YOU WITH
SIGH

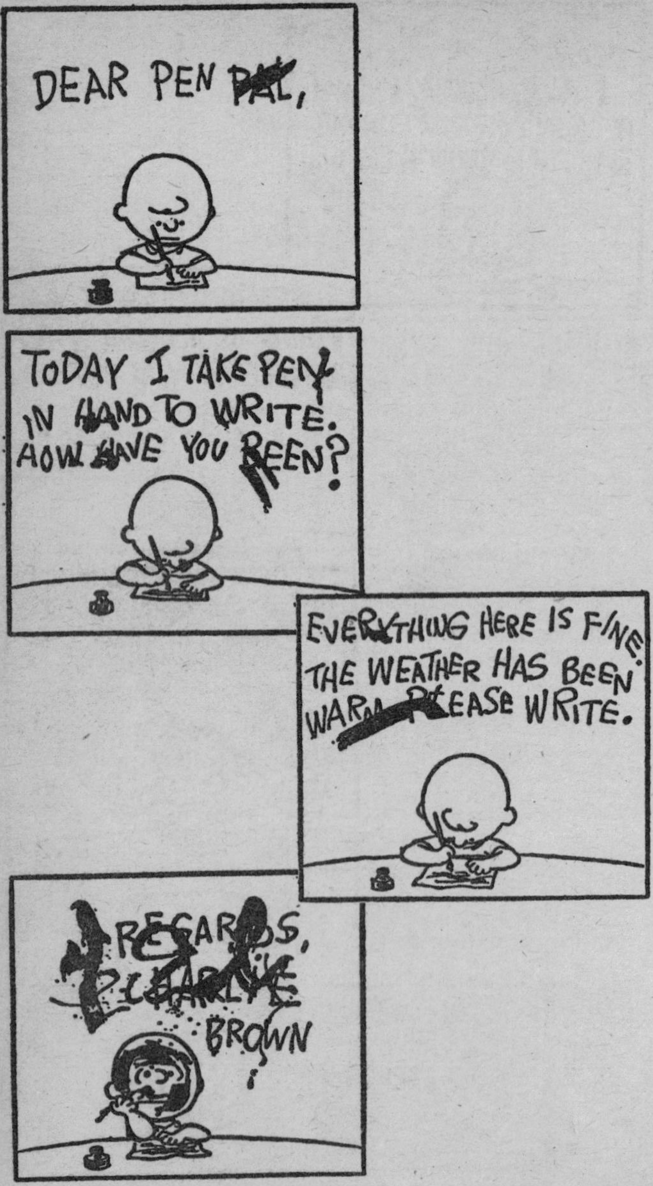
DEAR PEN PAL,
TODAY I TAKE PEN IN HAND TO WRITE. HOW HAVE YOU BEEN?
EVERYTHING HERE IS FINE. THE WEATHER HAS BEEN WARM PLEASE WRITE.
REGARDS,
CHARLIE
BROWN

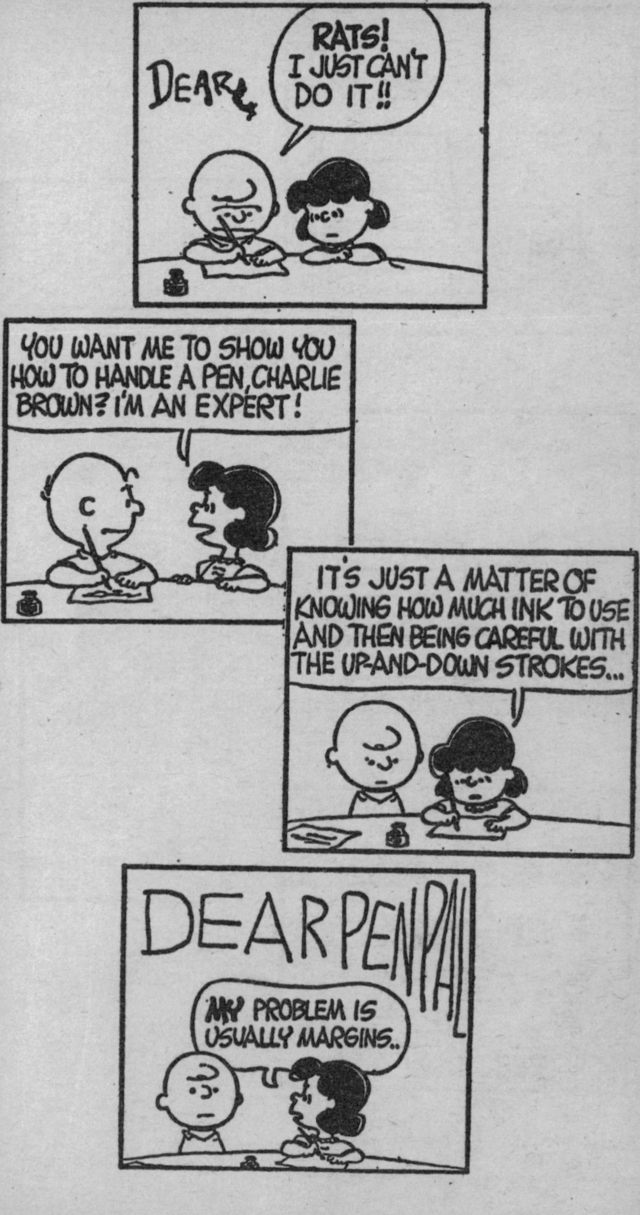
DEAR
RATS! I JUST CAN'T DO IT!!
YOU WANT ME TO SHOW YOU HOW TO HANDLE A PEN, CHARLIE BROWN? I'M AN EXPERT!
IT'S JUST A MATTER OF KNOWING HOW MUCH INK TO USE AND THEN BEING CAREFUL WITH THE UP-AND-DOWN STROKES...
DEAR PEN PAL
MY PROBLEM IS USUALLY MARGINS..

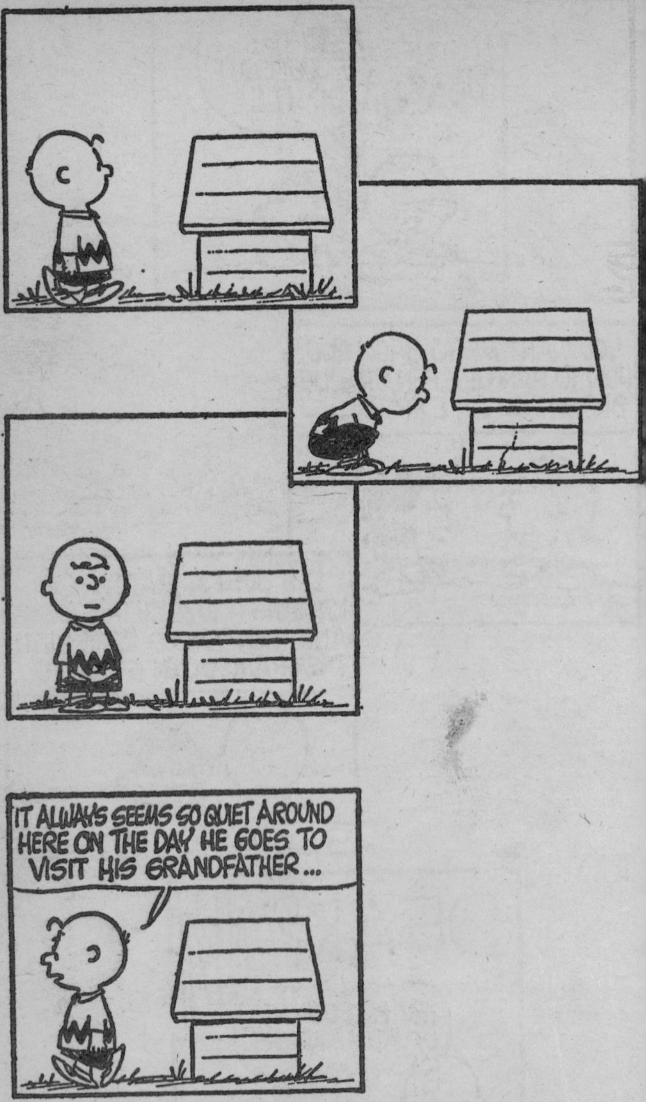
IT ALWAYS SEEMS SO QUIET AROUND HERE ON THE DAY HE GOES TO VISIT HIS GRANDFATHER...

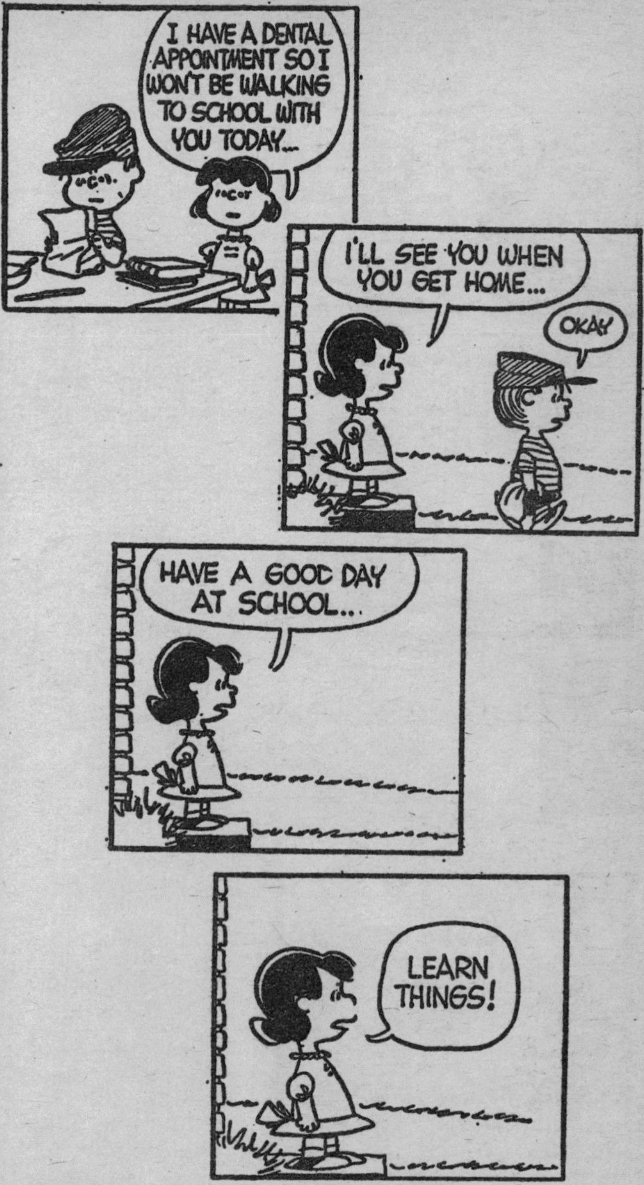
I HAVE A DENTAL APPOINTMENT SO I WON'T BE WALKING TO SCHOOL WITH YOU TODAY...
I'LL SEE YOU WHEN YOU GET HOME...
OKAY
HAVE A GOOD DAY AT SCHOOL...
LEARN THINGS!

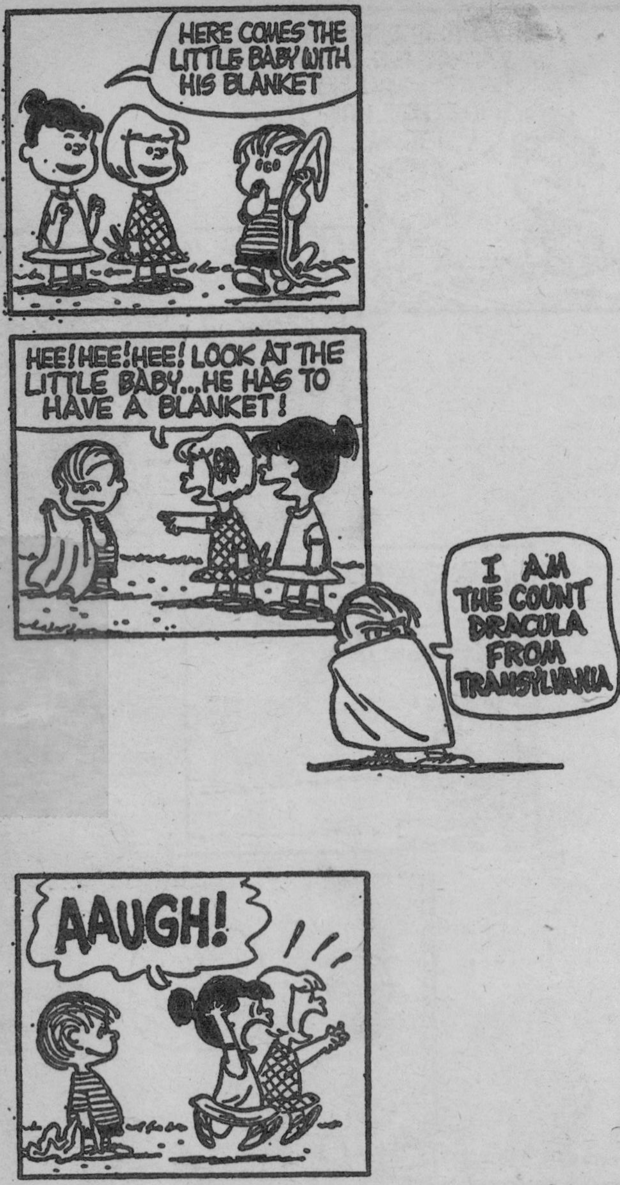
HERE COMES THE LITTLE BABY WITH HIS BLANKET
HEE! HEE! HEE! LOOK AT THE LITTLE BABY...HE HAS TO HAVE A BLANKET!
I AM THE COUNT DRACULA FROM TRANSYLVANIA
AAUGH!

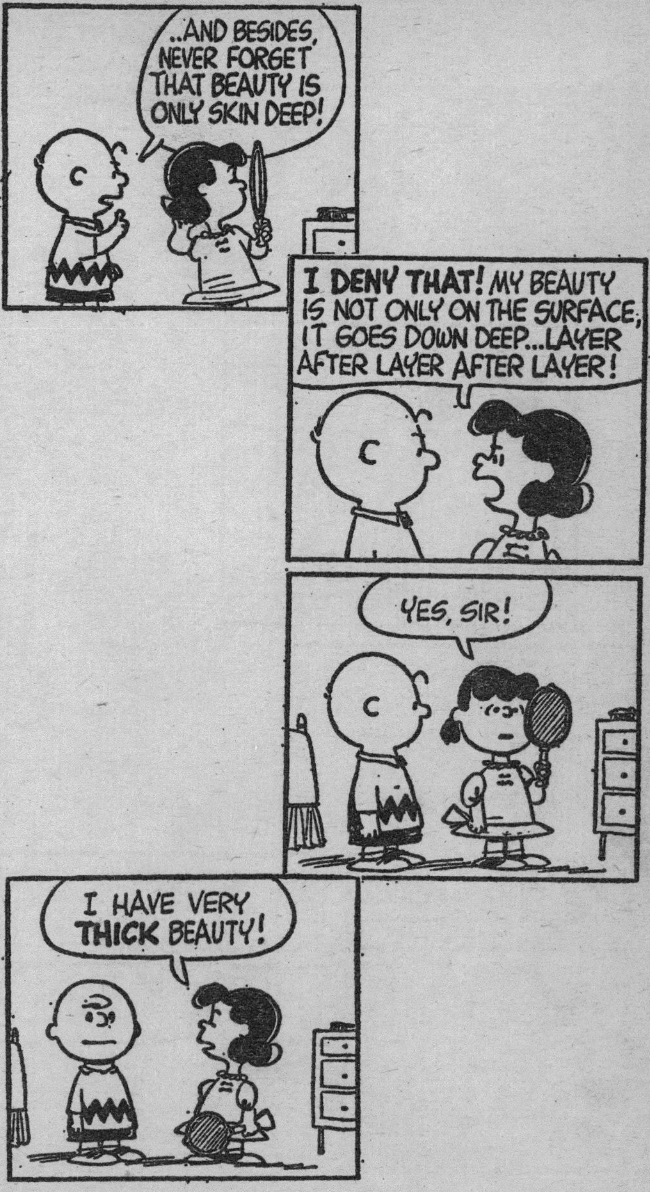
..AND BESIDES, NEVER FORGET THAT BEAUTY IS ONLY SKIN DEEP!
I DENY THAT! MY BEAUTY IS NOT ONLY ON THE SURFACE; IT GOES DOWN DEEP...LAYER AFTER LAYER AFTER LAYER!
YES, SIR!
I HAVE VERY THICK BEAUTY!

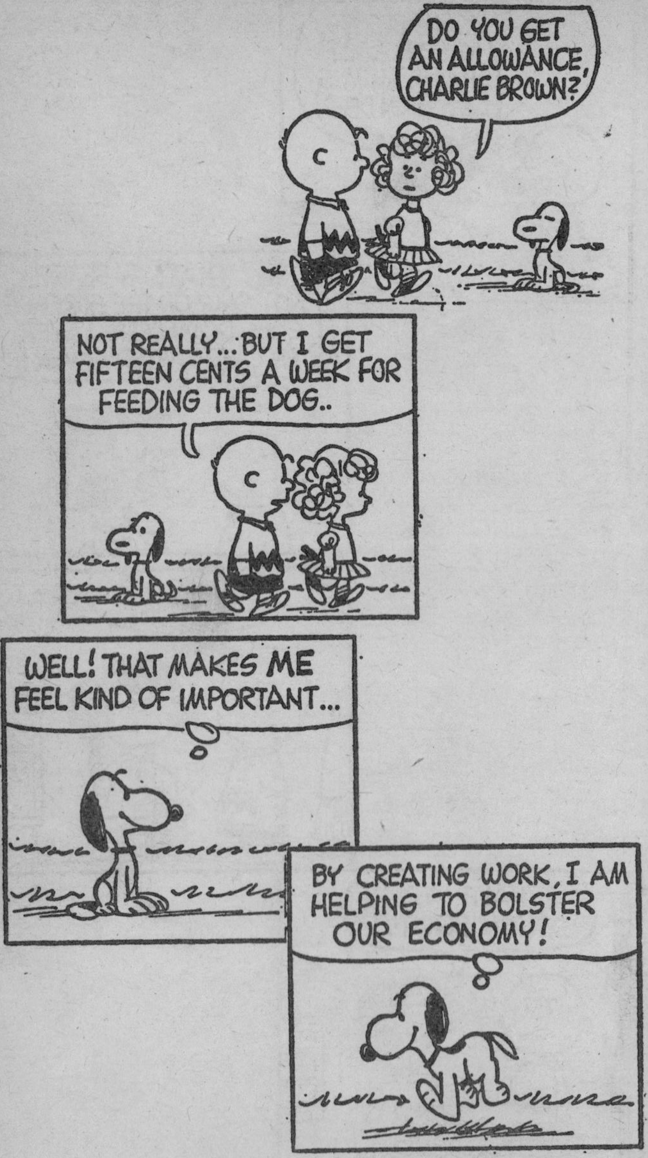
DO YOU GET AN ALLOWANCE, CHARLIE BROWN?
NOT REALLY...BUT I GET FIFTEEN CENTS A WEEK FOR FEEDING THE DOG..
WELL! THAT MAKES ME FEEL KIND OF IMPORTANT...
BY CREATING WORK, I AM HELPING TO BOLSTER OUR ECONOMY!

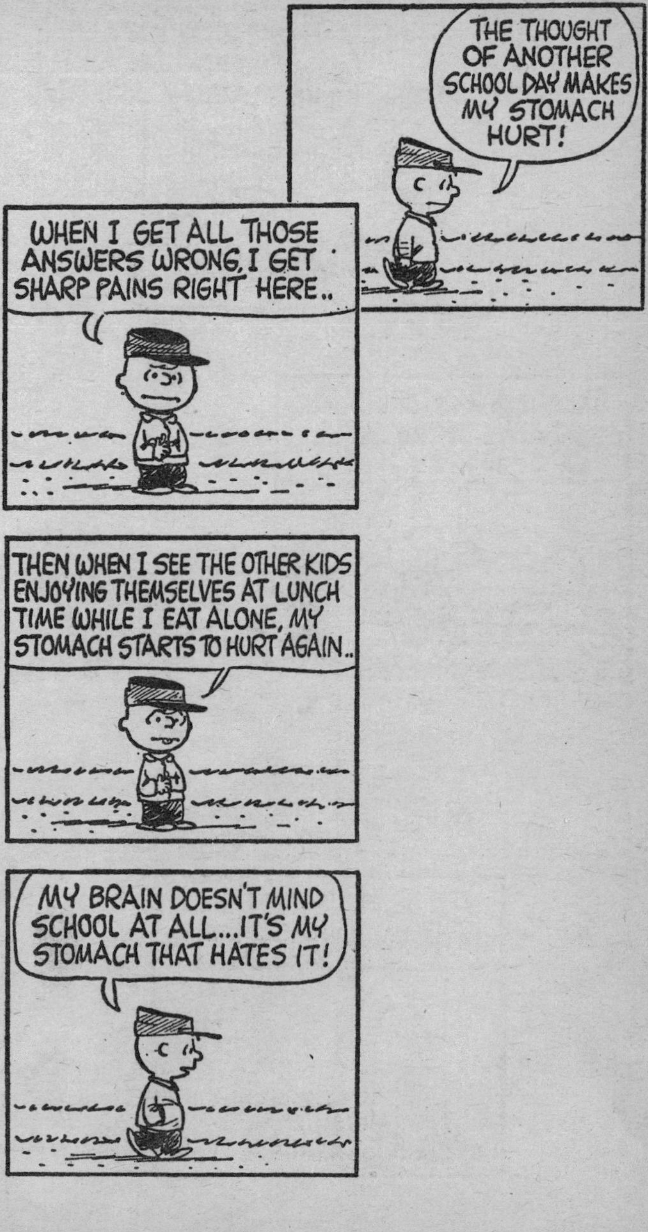
THE THOUGHT OF ANOTHER SCHOOL DAY MAKES MY STOMACH HURT!
WHEN I GET ALL THOSE ANSWERS WRONG, I GET SHARP PAINS RIGHT HERE..
THEN WHEN I SEE THE OTHER KIDS ENJOYING THEMSELVES AT LUNCH TIME WHILE I EAT ALONE, MY STOMACH STARTS TO HURT AGAIN..
MY BRAIN DOESN'T MIND SCHOOL AT ALL...IT'S MY STOMACH THAT HATES IT!

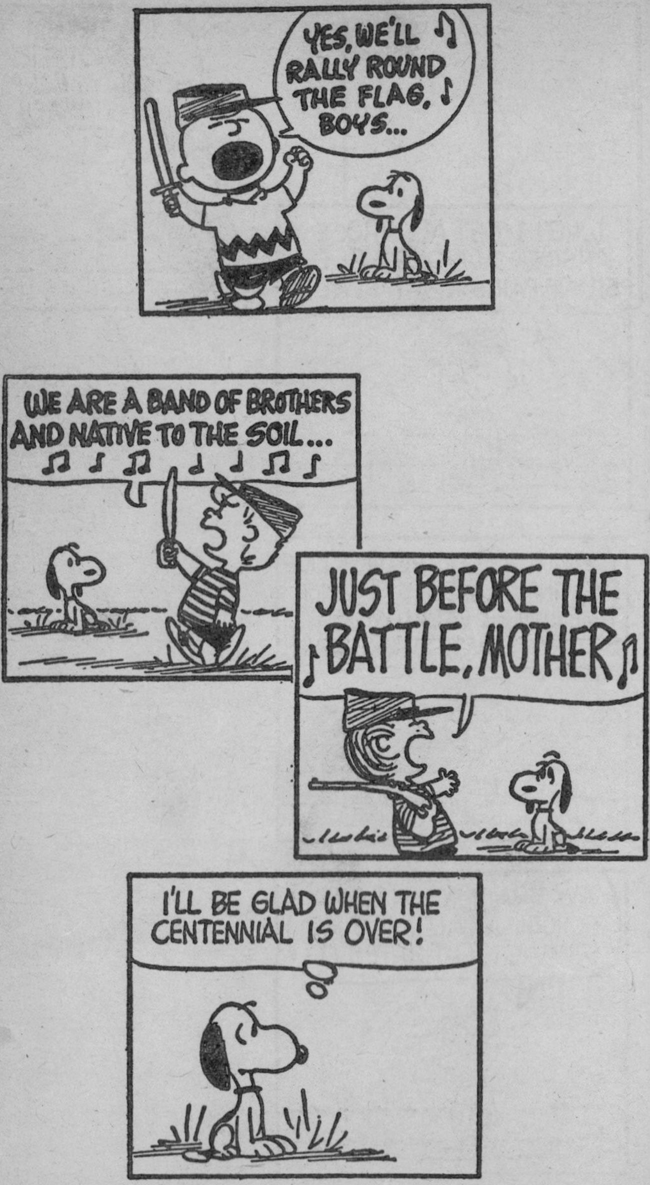
YES, WE'LL RALLY ROUND THE FLAG, BOYS...
WE ARE A BAND OF BROTHERS AND NATIVE TO THE SOIL...
JUST BEFORE THE BATTLE, MOTHER
I'LL BE GLAD WHEN THE CENTENNIAL IS OVER!

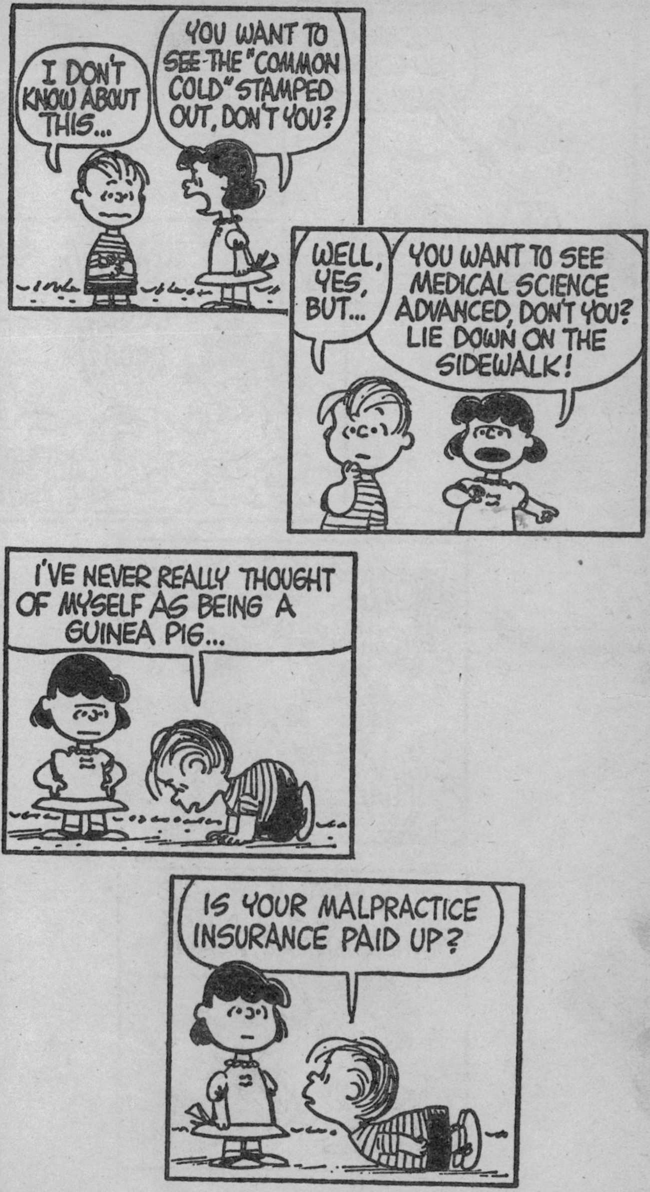
I DON'T KNOW ABOUT THIS...
YOU WANT TO SEE THE "COMMON COLD" STAMPED OUT, DON'T YOU?
WELL, YES, BUT...
YOU WANT TO SEE MEDICAL SCIENCE ADVANCED, DON'T YOU? LIE DOWN ON THE SIDEWALK!
I'VE NEVER REALLY THOUGHT OF MYSELF AS BEING A GUINEA PIG...
IS YOUR MALPRACTICE INSURANCE PAID UP?

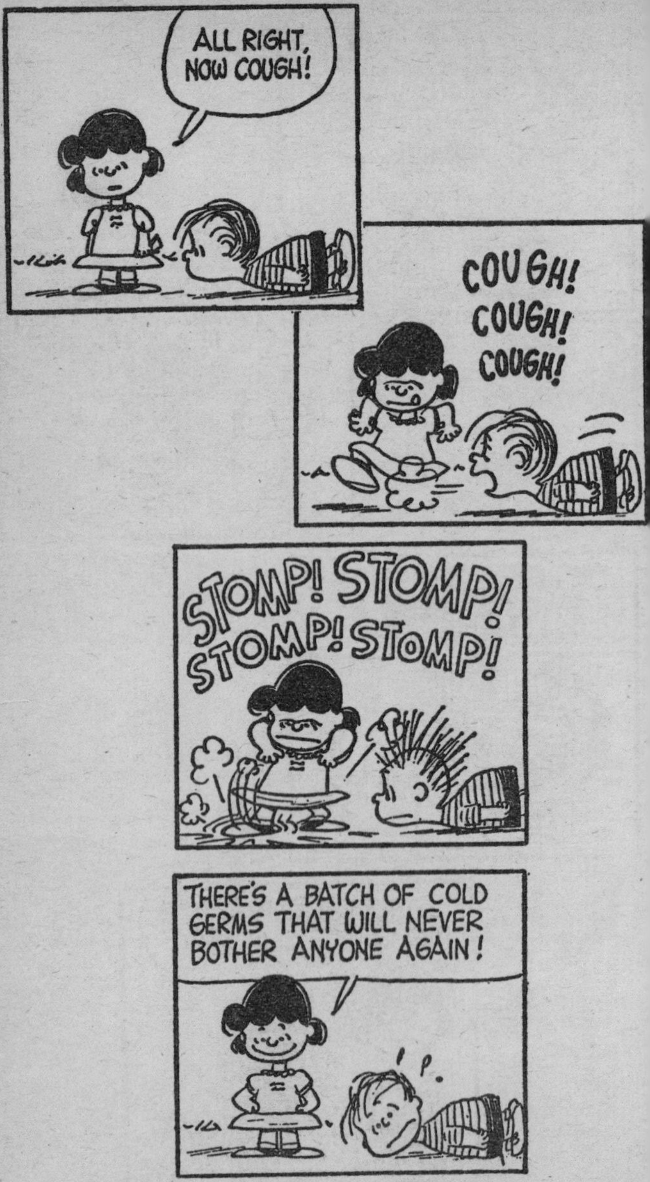
ALL RIGHT, NOW COUGH!
COUGH! COUGH! COUGH!
STOMP! STOMP! STOMP! STOMP!
THERE'S A BATCH OF COLD GERMS THAT WILL NEVER BOTHER ANYONE AGAIN!

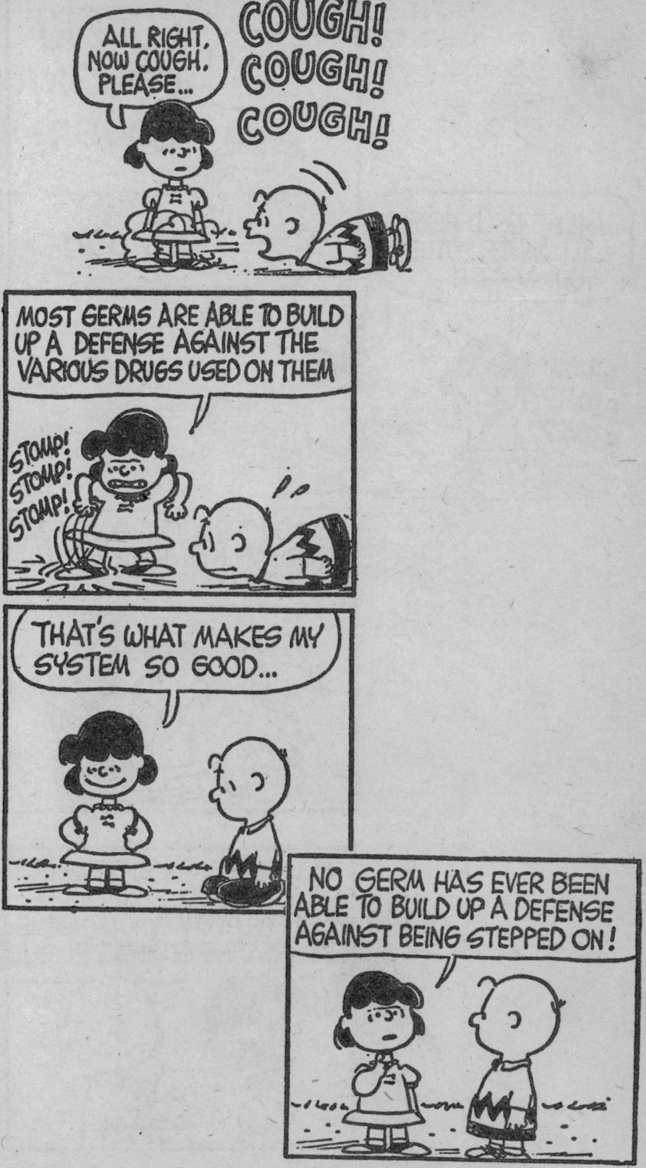
ALL RIGHT, NOW COUGH, PLEASE...
COUGH! COUGH! COUGH!
MOST GERMS ARE ABLE TO BUILD UP A DEFENSE AGAINST THE VARIOUS DRUGS USED ON THEM
STOMP! STOMP! STOMP!
THAT'S WHAT MAKES MY SYSTEM SO GOOD...
NO GERM HAS EVER BEEN ABLE TO BUILD UP A DEFENSE AGAINST BEING STEPPED ON!

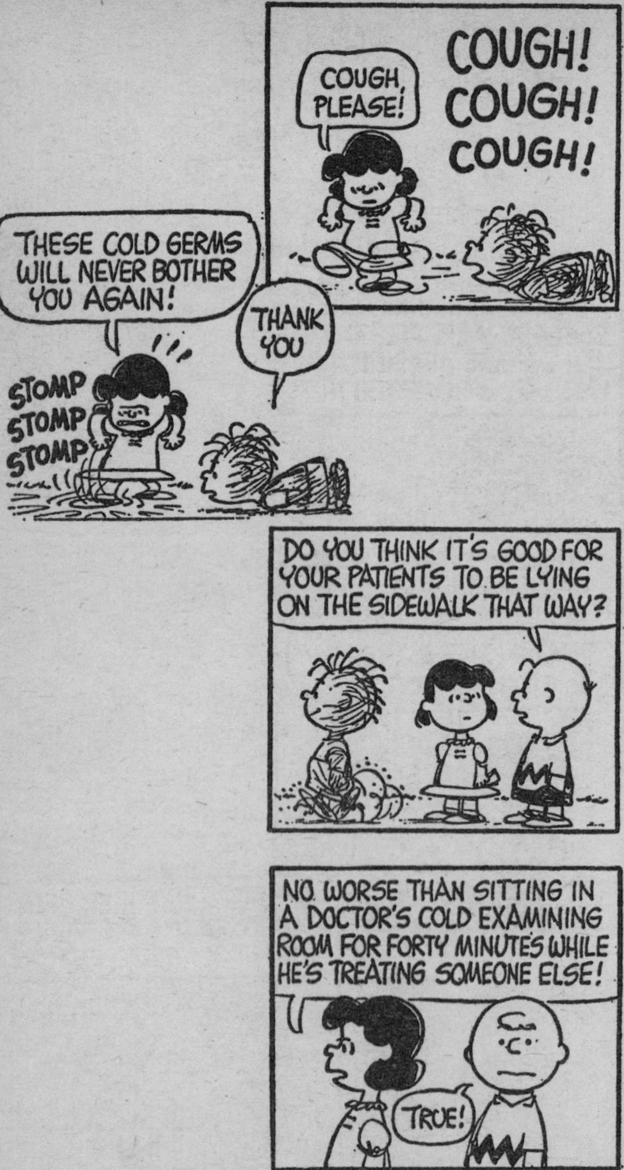
COUGH, PLEASE!
COUGH! COUGH! COUGH!
THESE COLD GERMS WILL NEVER BOTHER YOU AGAIN!
STOMP STOMP STOMP
THANK YOU
DO YOU THINK IT'S GOOD FOR YOUR PATIENTS TO BE LYING ON THE SIDEWALK THAT WAY?
NO WORSE THAN SITTING IN A DOCTOR'S COLD EXAMINING ROOM FOR FORTY MINUTES WHILE HE'S TREATING SOMEONE ELSE!
TRUE!

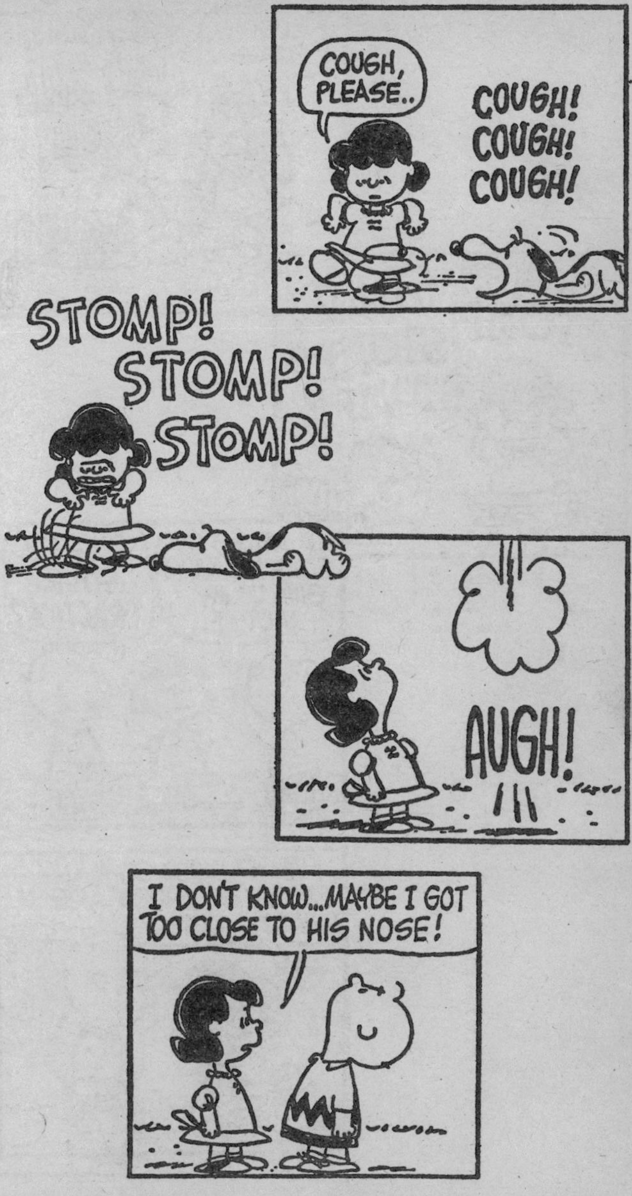
COUGH, PLEASE..
COUGH! COUGH! COUGH!
STOMP! STOMP! STOMP!
AUGH!
I DON'T KNOW...MAYBE I GOT TOO CLOSE TO HIS NOSE!

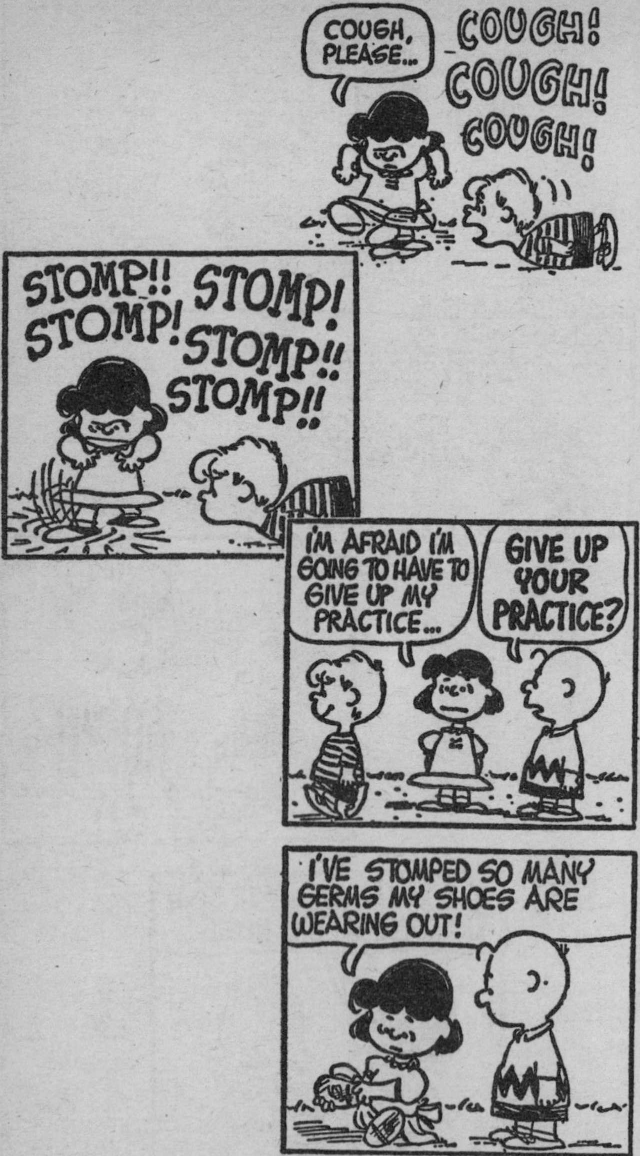
COUGH, PLEASE...
COUGH! COUGH! COUGH!
STOMP!! STOMP!
STOMP! STOMP!! STOMP!!
I'M AFRAID I'M GOING TO HAVE TO GIVE UP MY PRACTICE...
GIVE UP YOUR PRACTICE?
I'VE STOMPED SO MANY GERMS MY SHOES ARE WEARING OUT!

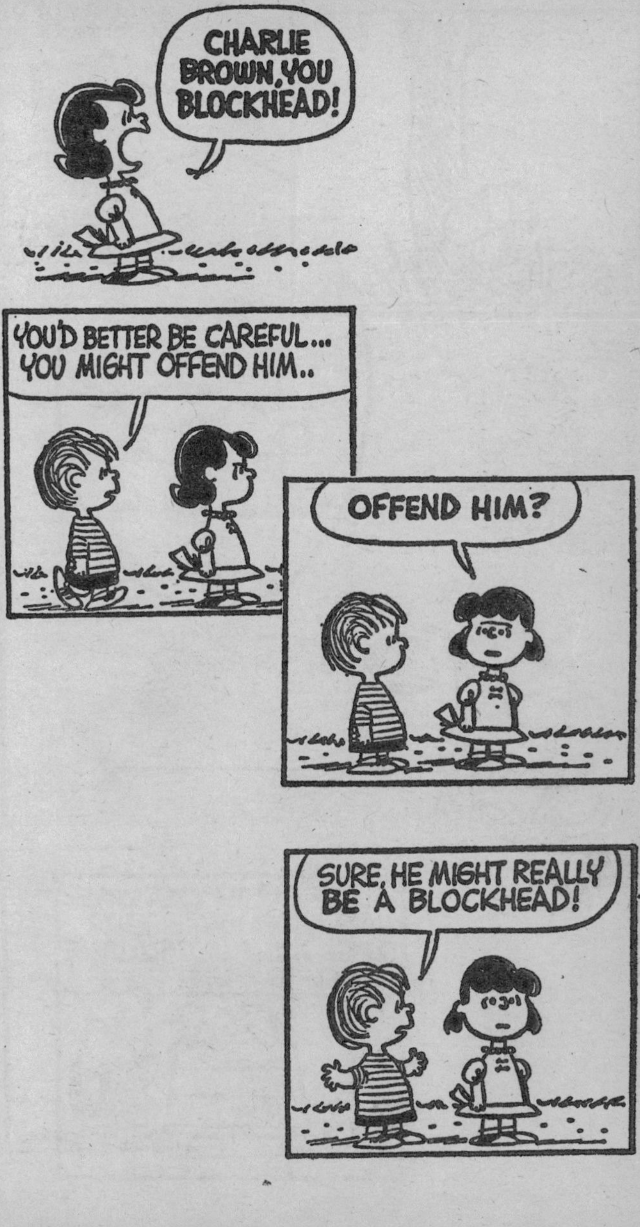
CHARLIE BROWN, YOU BLOCKHEAD!
YOU'D BETTER BE CAREFUL... YOU MIGHT OFFEND HIM..
OFFEND HIM?
SURE, HE MIGHT REALLY BE A BLOCKHEAD!

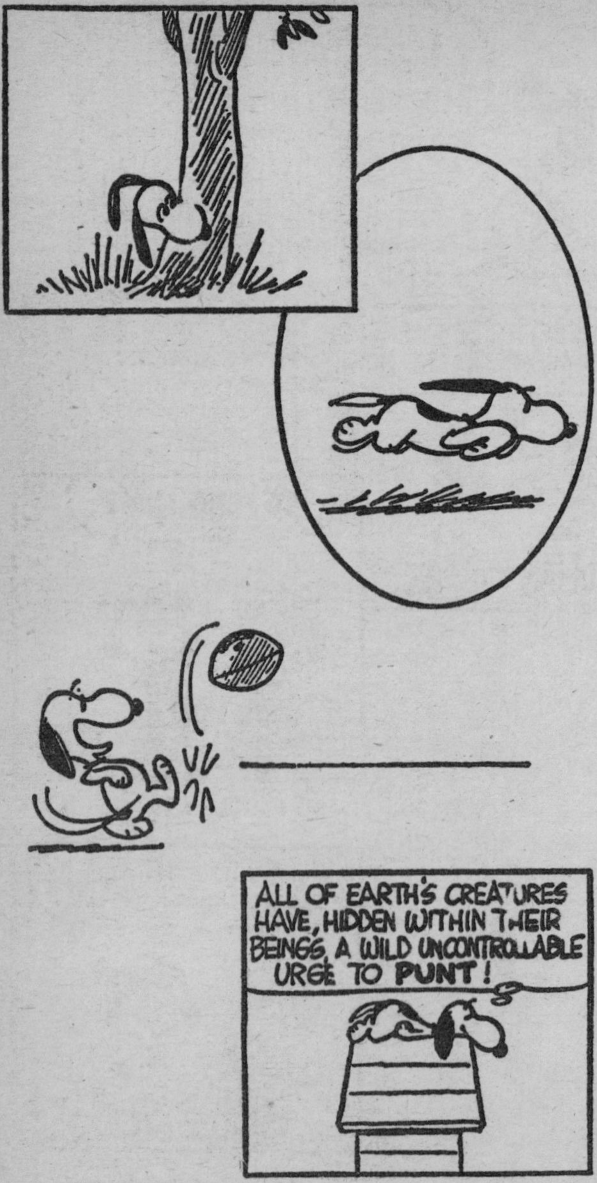

ALL OF EARTH'S CREATURES HAVE, HIDDEN WITHIN THEIR BEINGS, A WILD UNCONTROLLABLE URGE TO PUNT!

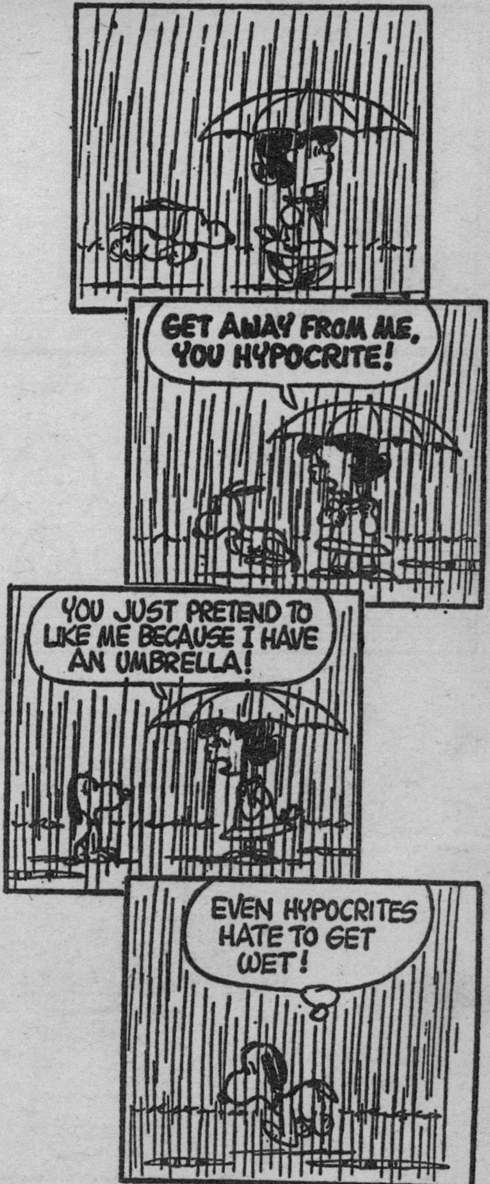
GET AWAY FROM ME, YOU HYPOCRITE!
YOU JUST PRETEND TO LIKE ME BECAUSE I HAVE AN UMBRELLA!
EVEN HYPOCRITES HATE TO GET WET!

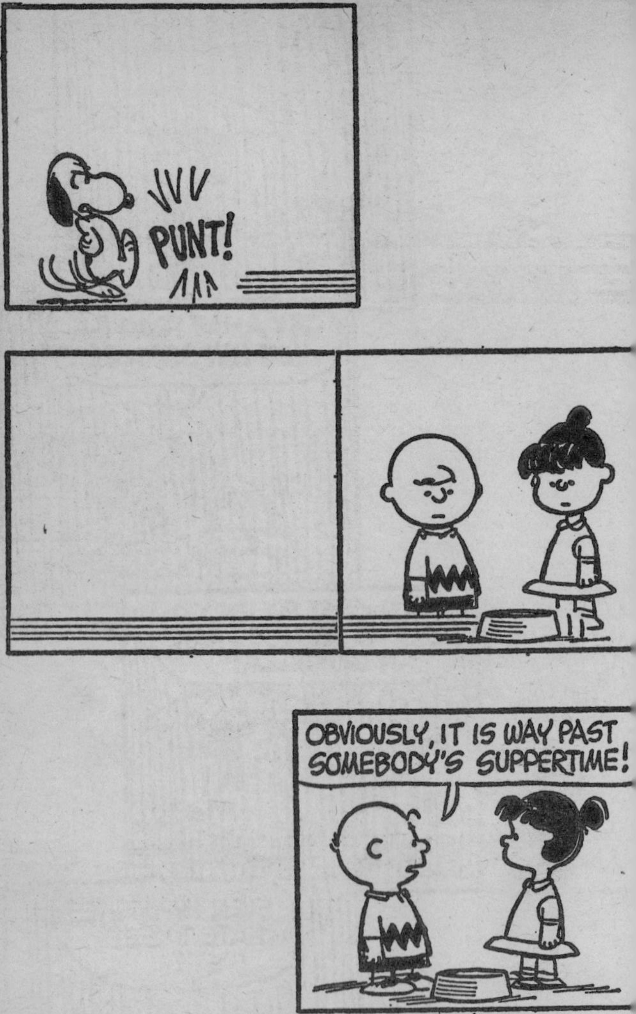
PUNT!
OBVIOUSLY, IT IS WAY PAST SOMEBODY'S SUPPERTIME!

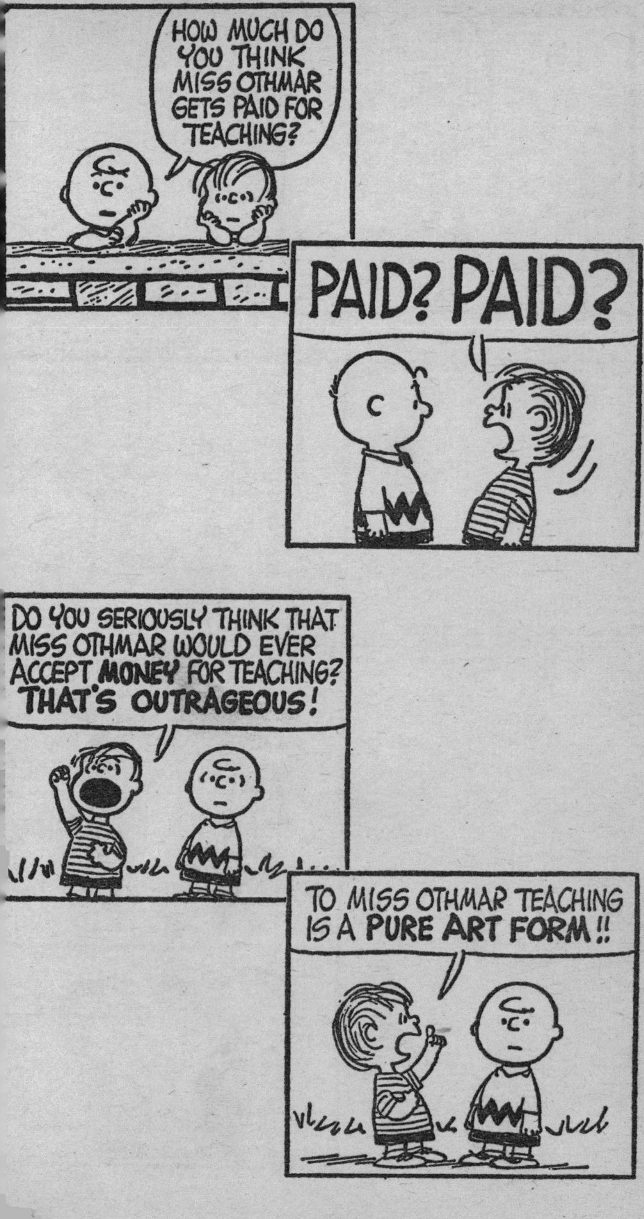
HOW MUCH DO YOU THINK MISS OTHMAR GETS PAID FOR TEACHING?
PAID? PAID?
DO YOU SERIOUSLY THINK THAT MISS OTHMAR WOULD EVER ACCEPT MONEY FOR TEACHING? THAT'S OUTRAGEOUS!
TO MISS OTHMAR TEACHING IS A PURE ART FORM!!

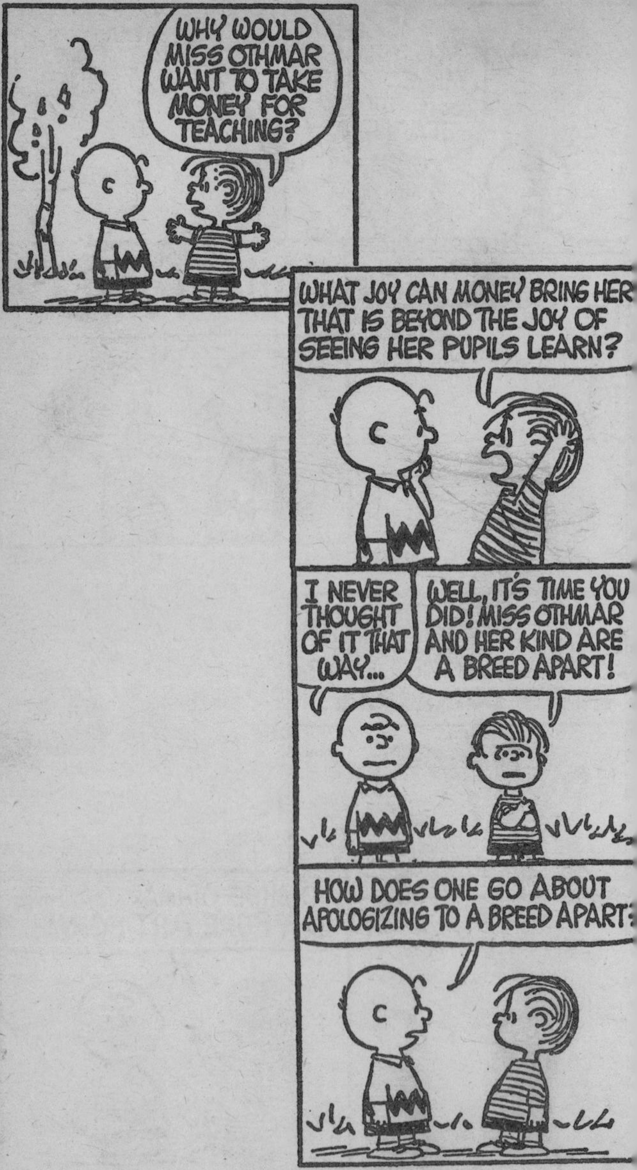
WHY WOULD MISS OTHMAR WANT TO TAKE MONEY FOR TEACHING?
WHAT JOY CAN MONEY BRING HER THAT IS BEYOND THE JOY OF SEEING HER PUPILS LEARN?
I NEVER THOUGHT OF IT THAT WAY...
WELL, IT'S TIME YOU DID! MISS OTHMAR AND HER KIND ARE A BREED APART!
HOW DOES ONE GO ABOUT APOLOGIZING TO A BREED APART?

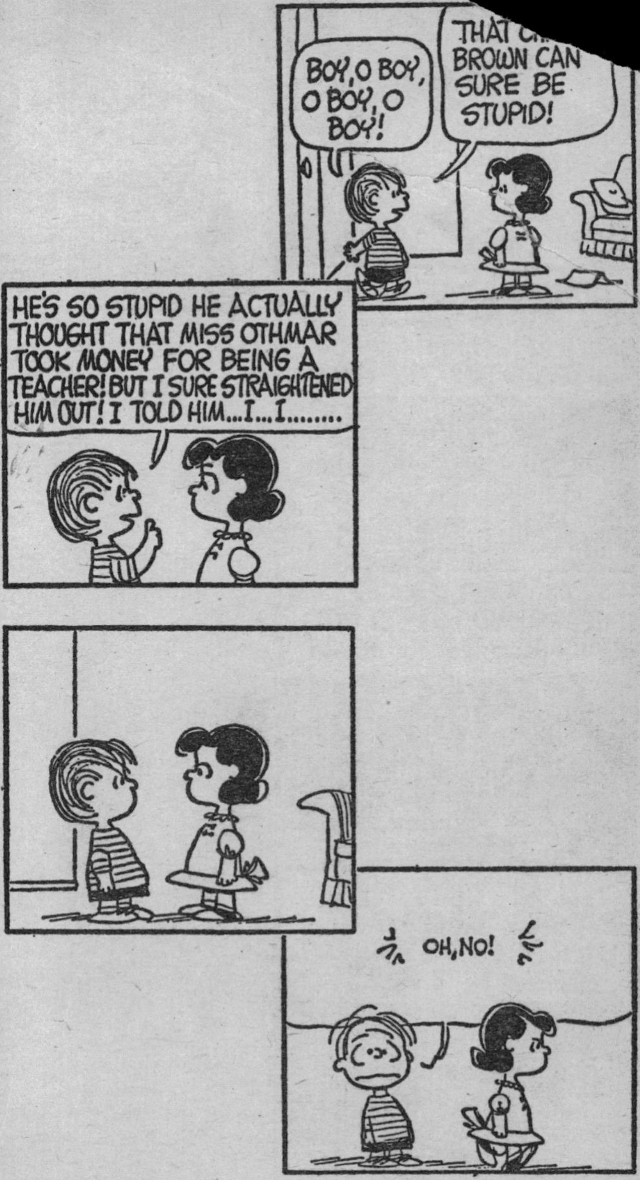
BOY, O BOY, O BOY, O BOY!
THAT
BROWN CAN SURE BE STUPID!
HE'S SO STUPID HE ACTUALLY THOUGHT THAT MISS OTHMAR TOOK MONEY FOR BEING A TEACHER! BUT I SURE STRAIGHTENED HIM OUT! I TOLD HIM...I...I........
OH, NO!

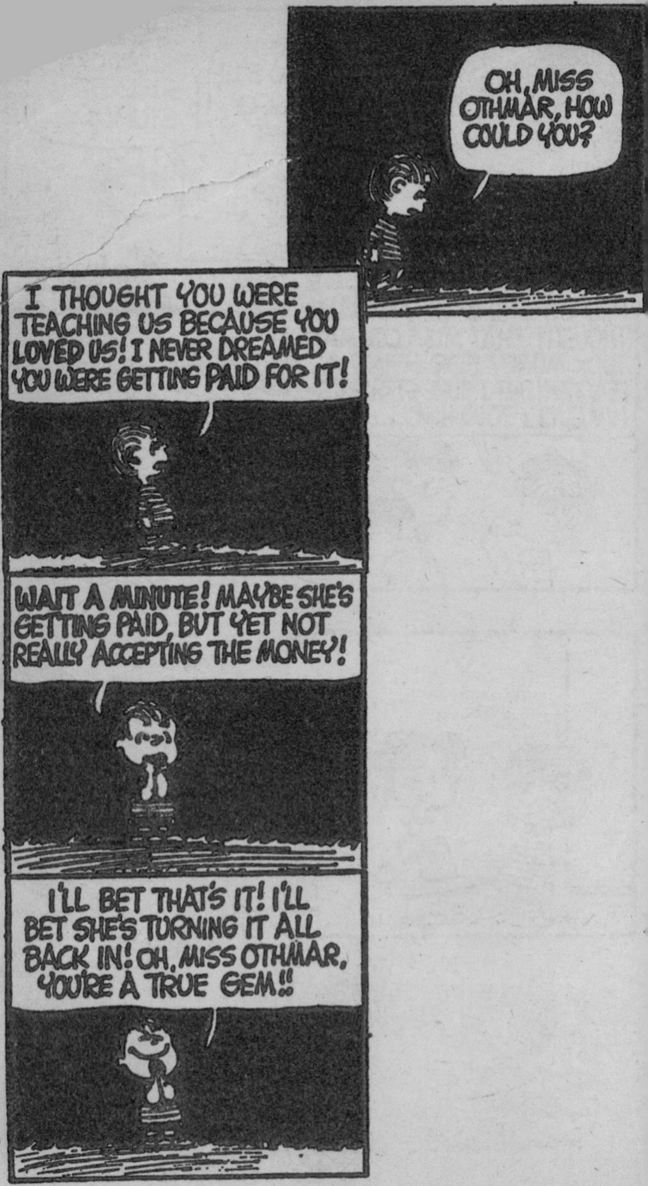
OH, MISS OTHMAR, HOW COULD YOU?
I THOUGHT YOU WERE TEACHING US BECAUSE YOU LOVED US! I NEVER DREAMED YOU WERE GETTING PAID FOR IT!
WAIT A MINUTE! MAYBE SHE'S GETTING PAID, BUT YET NOT REALLY ACCEPTING THE MONEY!
I'LL BET THAT'S IT! I'LL BET SHE'S TURNING IT ALL BACK IN! OH, MISS OTHMAR, YOU'RE A TRUE GEM!!

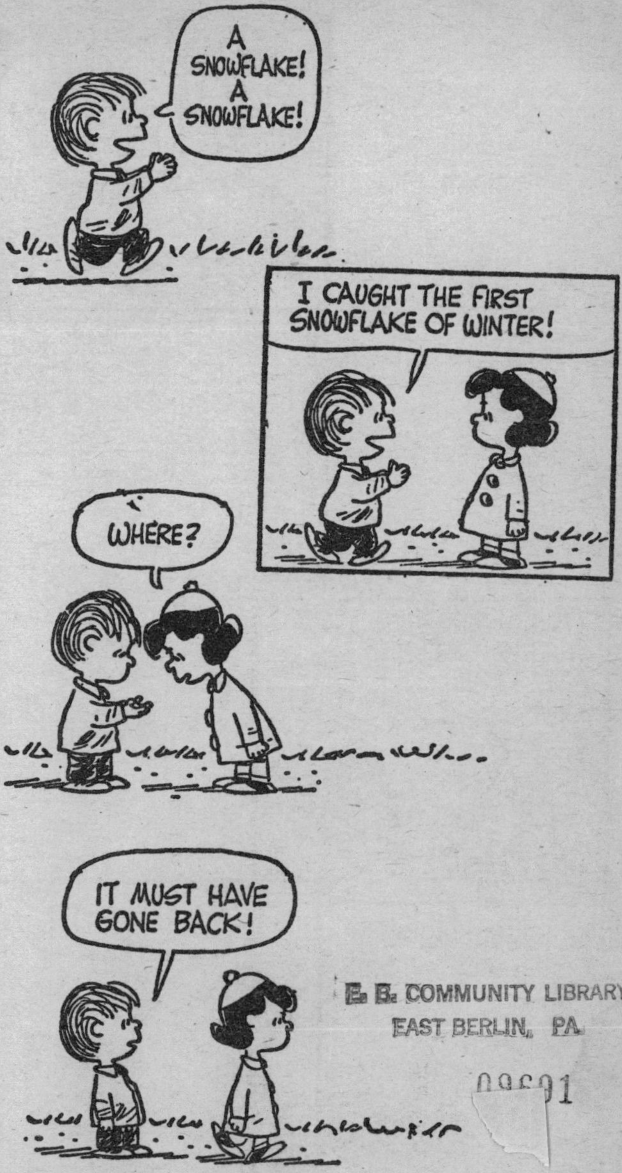
A SNOWFLAKE! A SNOWFLAKE!
I CAUGHT THE FIRST SNOWFLAKE OF WINTER!
WHERE?
IT MUST HAVE GONE BACK!

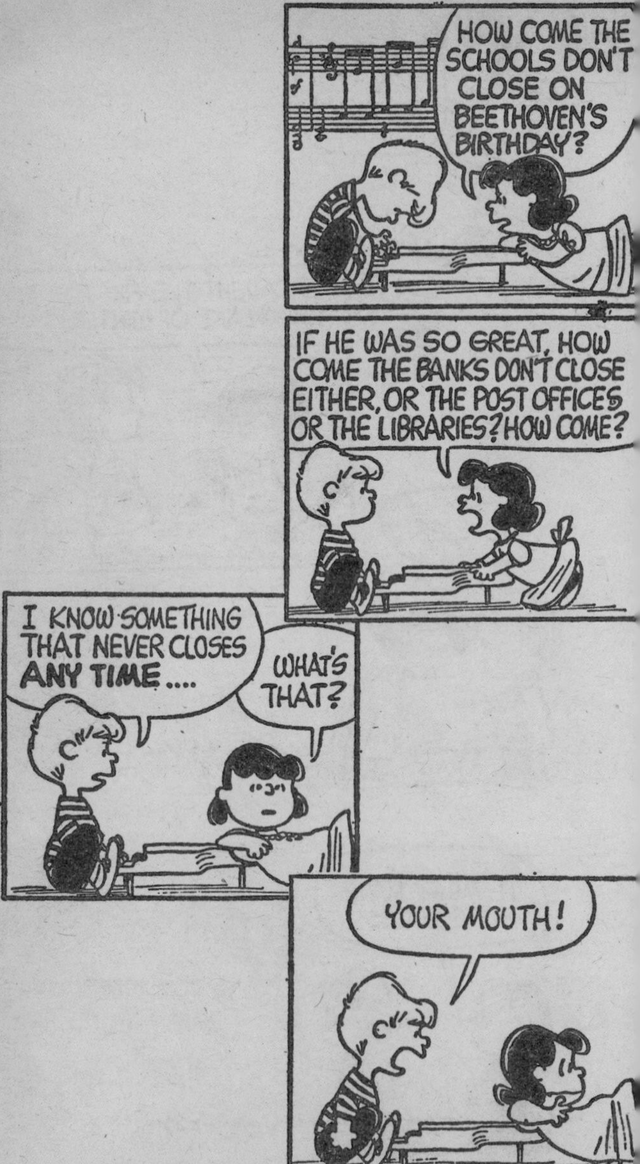
HOW COME THE SCHOOLS DON'T CLOSE ON BEETHOVEN'S BIRTHDAY?
IF HE WAS SO GREAT, HOW COME THE BANKS DON'T CLOSE EITHER, OR THE POST OFFICES OR THE LIBRARIES? HOW COME?
I KNOW SOMETHING THAT NEVER CLOSES **ANY TIME**....
WHAT'S THAT?
YOUR MOUTH!

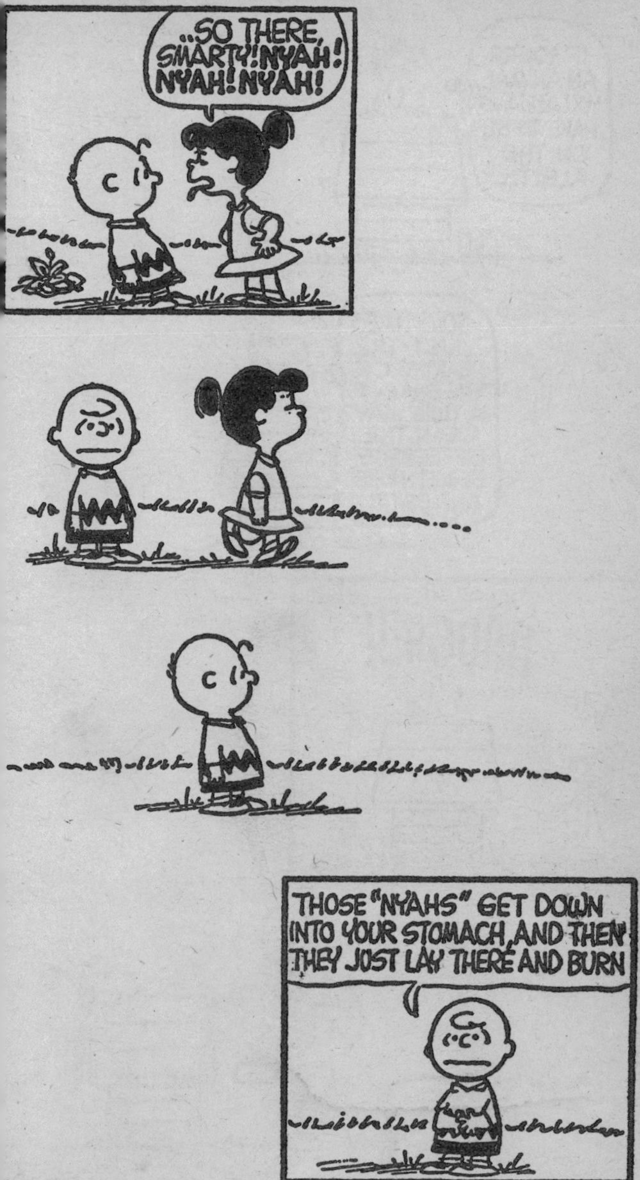
..SO THERE, SMARTY! NYAH! NYAH! NYAH!
THOSE "NYAHS" GET DOWN INTO YOUR STOMACH, AND THEN THEY JUST LAY THERE AND BURN

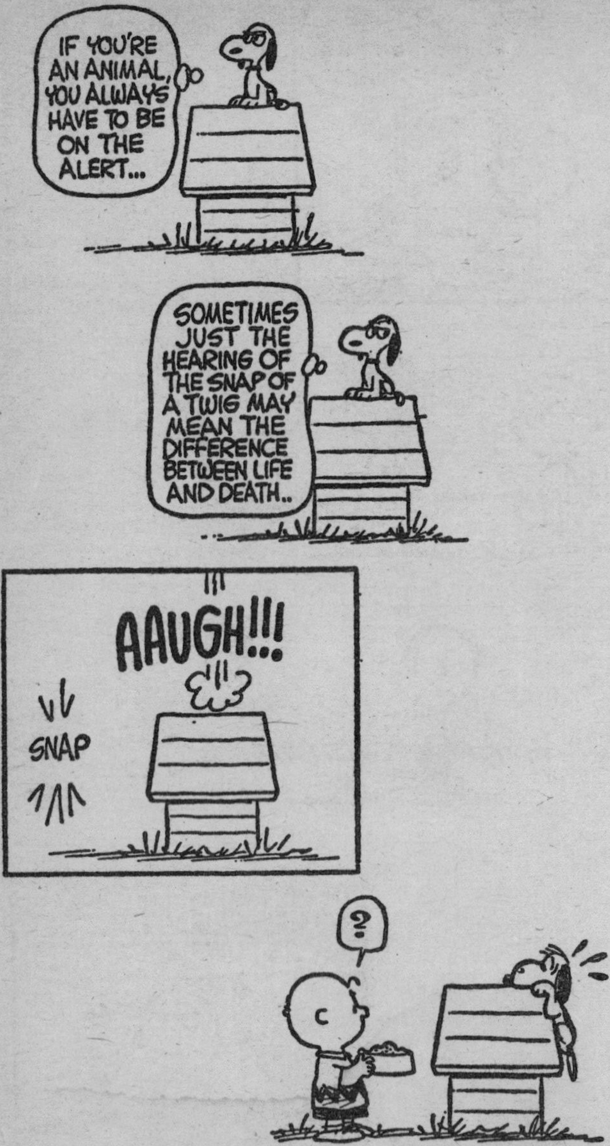
IF YOU'RE AN ANIMAL, YOU ALWAYS HAVE TO BE ON THE ALERT...
SOMETIMES JUST THE HEARING OF THE SNAP OF A TWIG MAY MEAN THE DIFFERENCE BETWEEN LIFE AND DEATH..
AAUGH!!!
SNAP
?

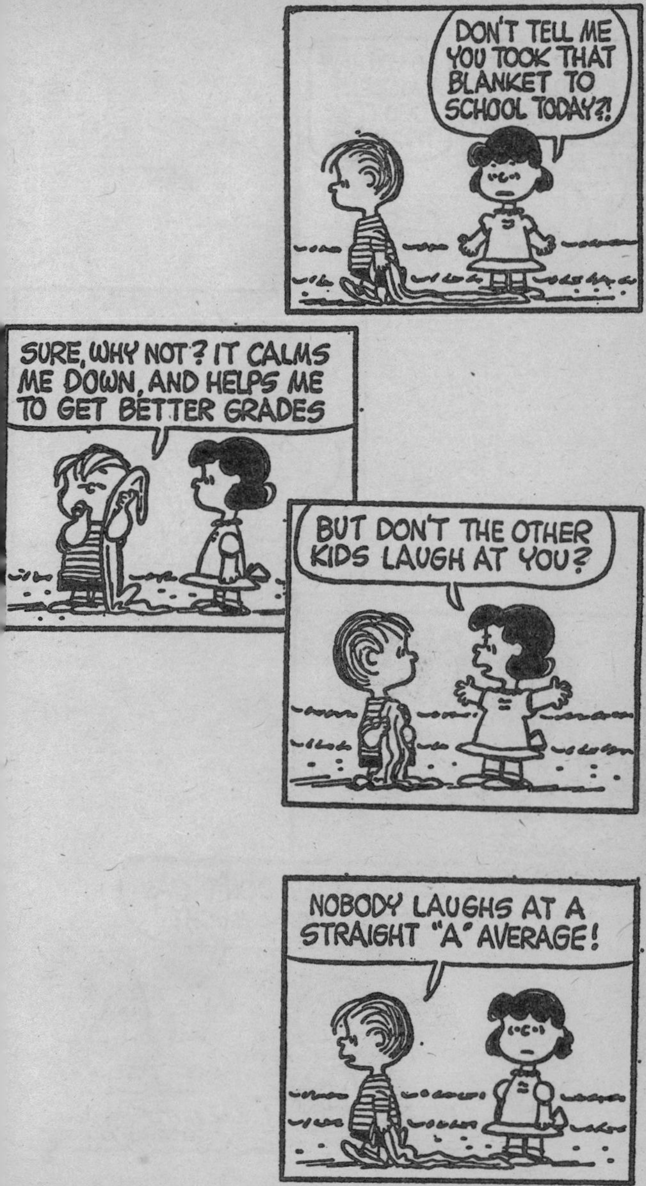
DON'T TELL ME YOU TOOK THAT BLANKET TO SCHOOL TODAY?!
SURE, WHY NOT? IT CALMS ME DOWN, AND HELPS ME TO GET BETTER GRADES
BUT DON'T THE OTHER KIDS LAUGH AT YOU?
NOBODY LAUGHS AT A STRAIGHT "A" AVERAGE!

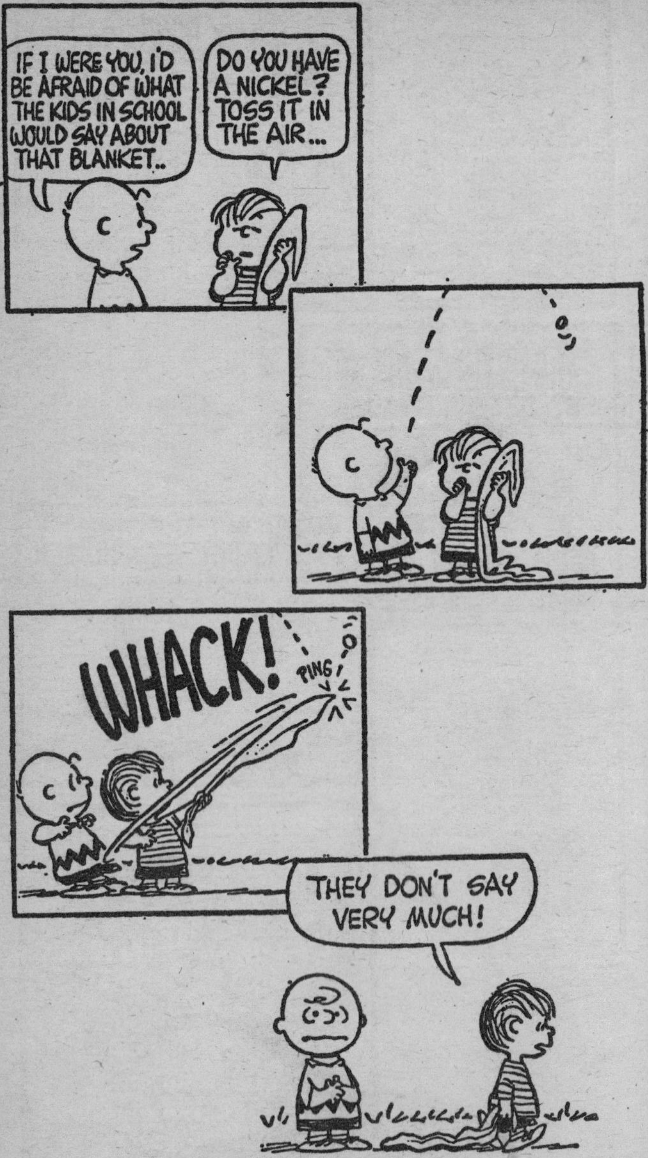
IF I WERE YOU, I'D BE AFRAID OF WHAT THE KIDS IN SCHOOL WOULD SAY ABOUT THAT BLANKET..
DO YOU HAVE A NICKEL? TOSS IT IN THE AIR...
WHACK!
PING
THEY DON'T SAY VERY MUCH!

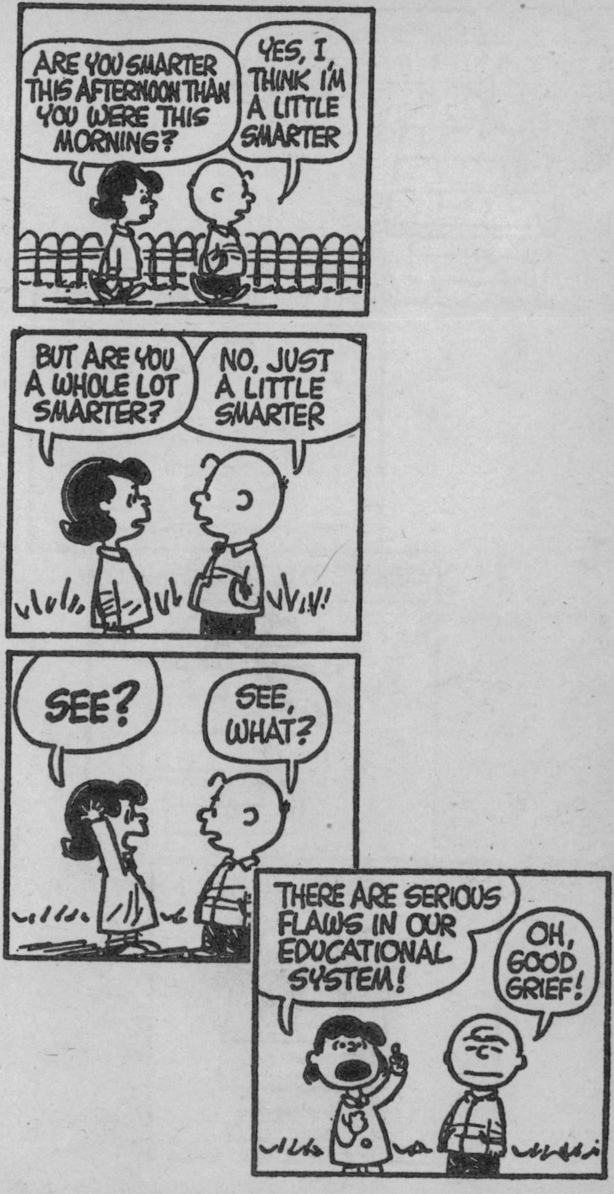
ARE YOU SMARTER THIS AFTERNOON THAN YOU WERE THIS MORNING?
YES, I THINK I'M A LITTLE SMARTER
BUT ARE YOU A WHOLE LOT SMARTER?
NO, JUST A LITTLE SMARTER
SEE?
SEE, WHAT?
THERE ARE SERIOUS FLAWS IN OUR EDUCATIONAL SYSTEM!
OH, GOOD GRIEF!

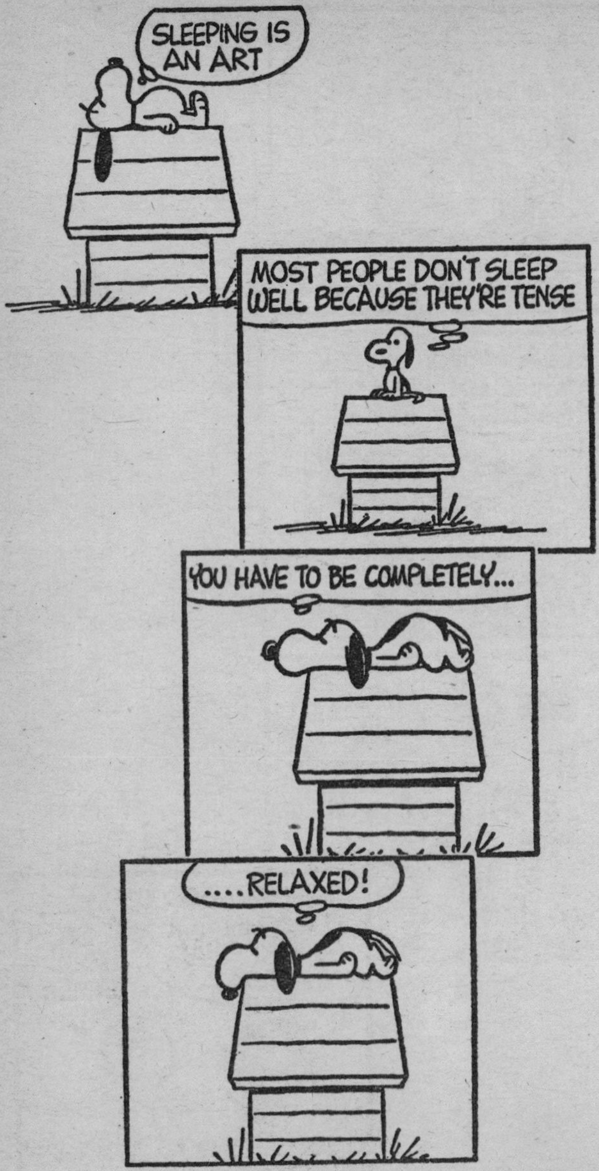
SLEEPING IS AN ART
MOST PEOPLE DON'T SLEEP WELL BECAUSE THEY'RE TENSE
YOU HAVE TO BE COMPLETELY...
....RELAXED!

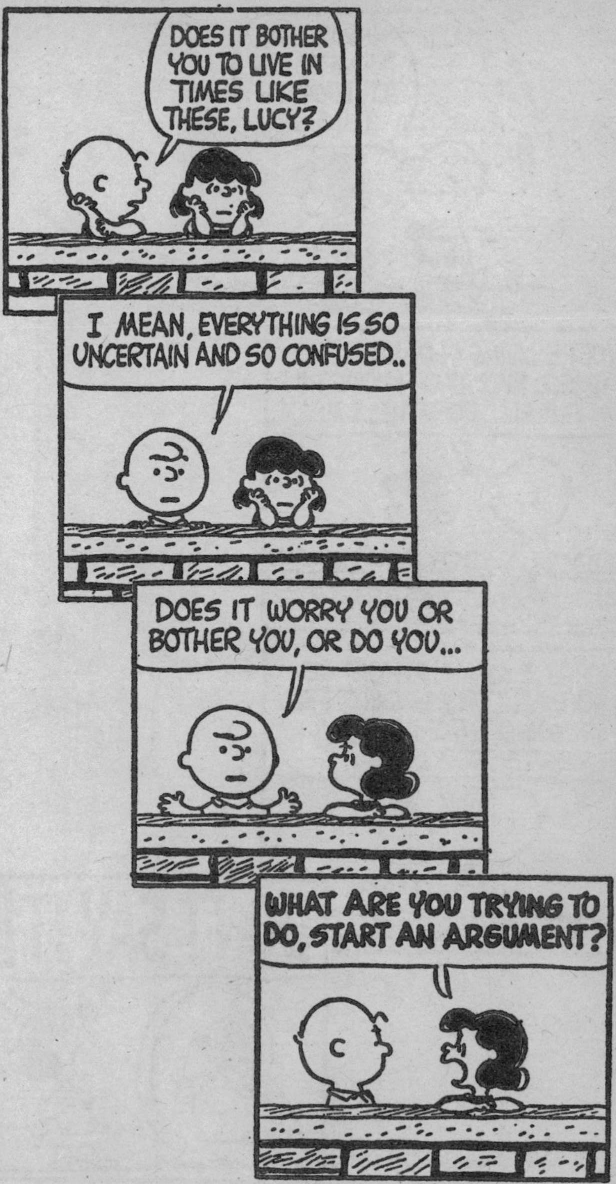
DOES IT BOTHER YOU TO LIVE IN TIMES LIKE THESE, LUCY?
I MEAN, EVERYTHING IS SO UNCERTAIN AND SO CONFUSED..
DOES IT WORRY YOU OR BOTHER YOU, OR DO YOU...
WHAT ARE YOU TRYING TO DO, START AN ARGUMENT?

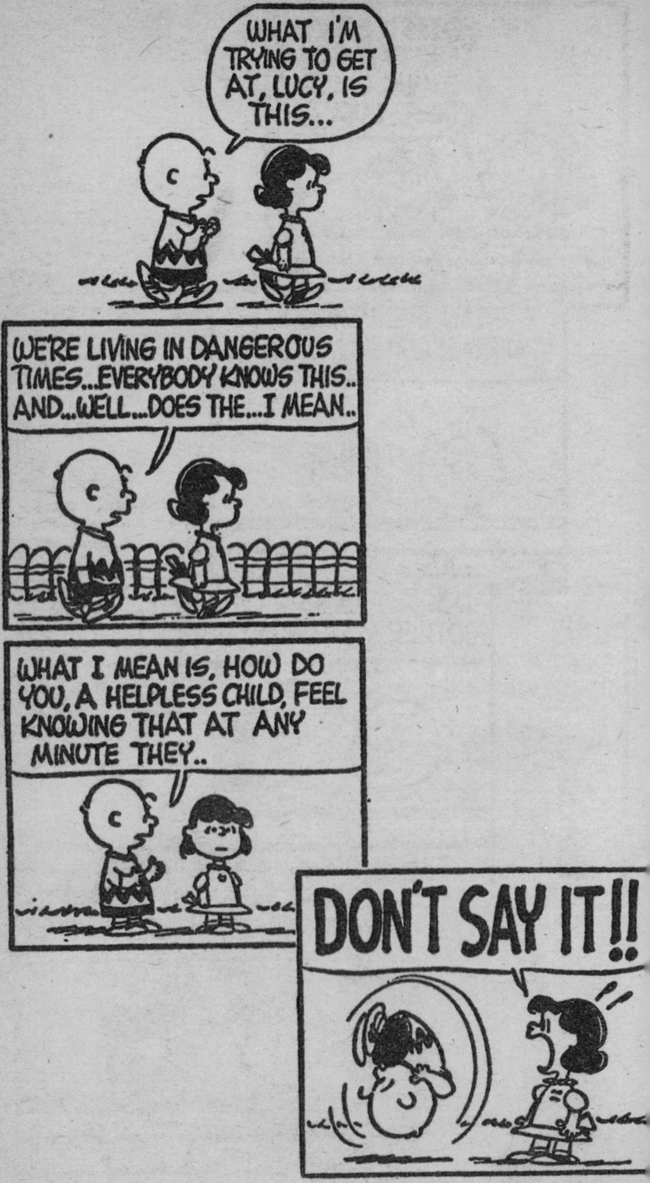
WHAT I'M TRYING TO GET AT, LUCY, IS THIS...
WE'RE LIVING IN DANGEROUS TIMES...EVERYBODY KNOWS THIS.. AND...WELL...DOES THE...I MEAN..
WHAT I MEAN IS, HOW DO YOU, A HELPLESS CHILD, FEEL KNOWING THAT AT ANY MINUTE THEY..
DON'T SAY IT!!

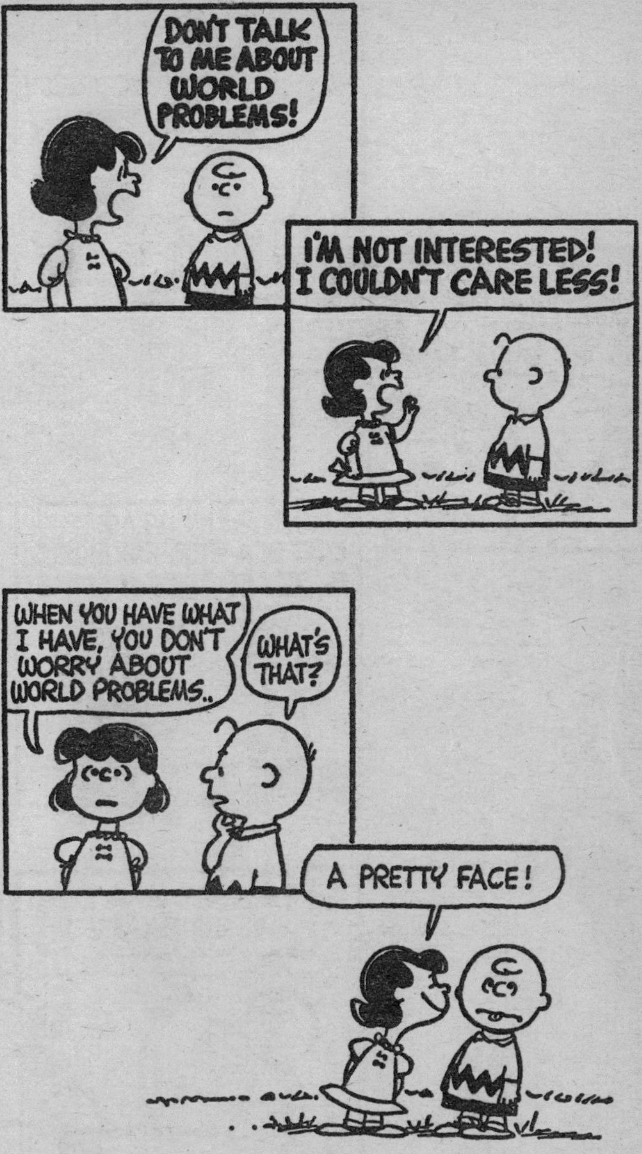
DON'T TALK TO ME ABOUT WORLD PROBLEMS!
I'M NOT INTERESTED! I COULDN'T CARE LESS!
WHEN YOU HAVE WHAT I HAVE, YOU DON'T WORRY ABOUT WORLD PROBLEMS..
WHAT'S THAT?
A PRETTY FACE!

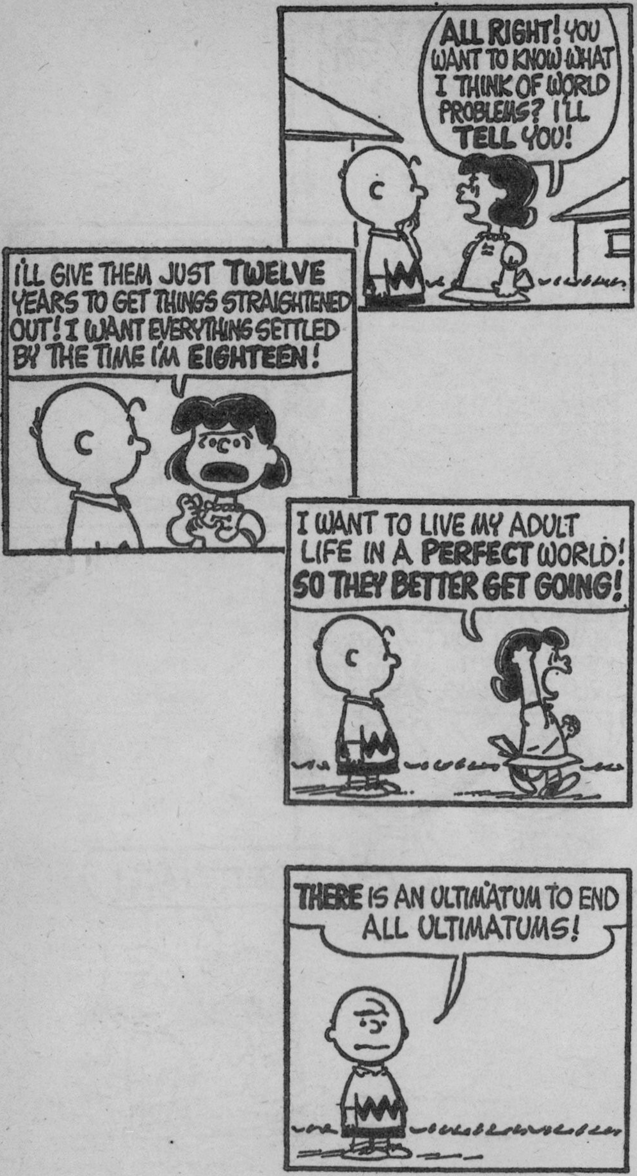
ALL RIGHT! YOU WANT TO KNOW WHAT I THINK OF WORLD PROBLEMS? I'LL TELL YOU!
I'LL GIVE THEM JUST TWELVE YEARS TO GET THINGS STRAIGHTENED OUT! I WANT EVERYTHING SETTLED BY THE TIME I'M EIGHTEEN!
I WANT TO LIVE MY ADULT LIFE IN A PERFECT WORLD! SO THEY BETTER GET GOING!
THERE IS AN ULTIMATUM TO END ALL ULTIMATUMS!

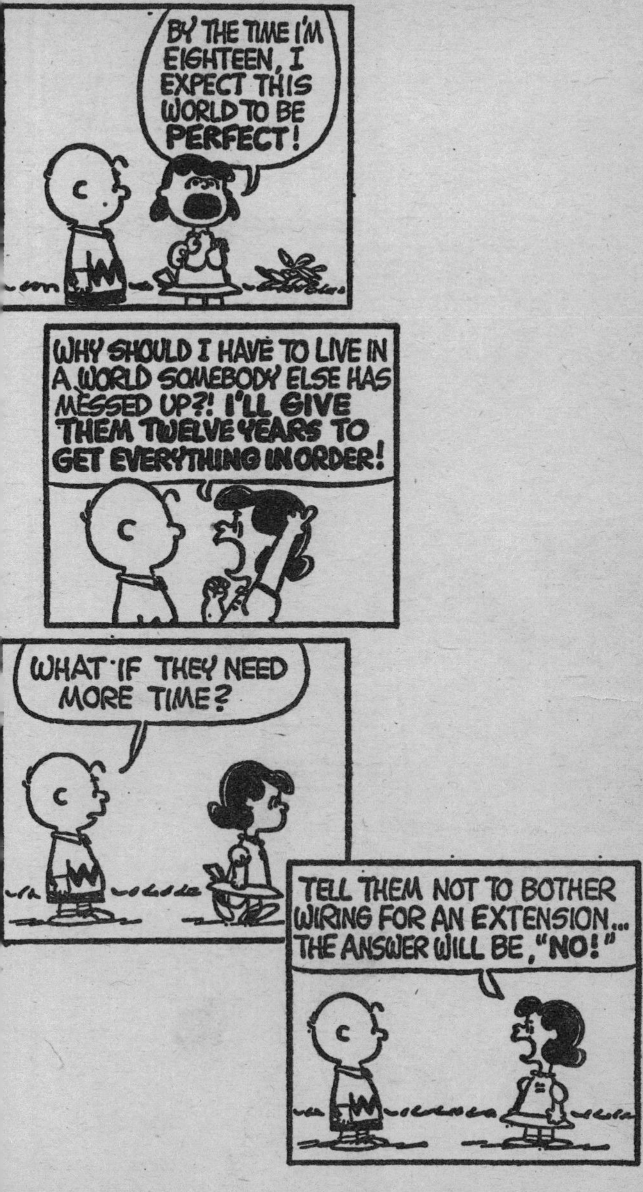
BY THE TIME I'M EIGHTEEN, I EXPECT THIS WORLD TO BE PERFECT!
WHY SHOULD I HAVE TO LIVE IN A WORLD SOMEBODY ELSE HAS MESSED UP?! I'LL GIVE THEM TWELVE YEARS TO GET EVERYTHING IN ORDER!
WHAT IF THEY NEED MORE TIME?
TELL THEM NOT TO BOTHER WIRING FOR AN EXTENSION... THE ANSWER WILL BE, "NO!"

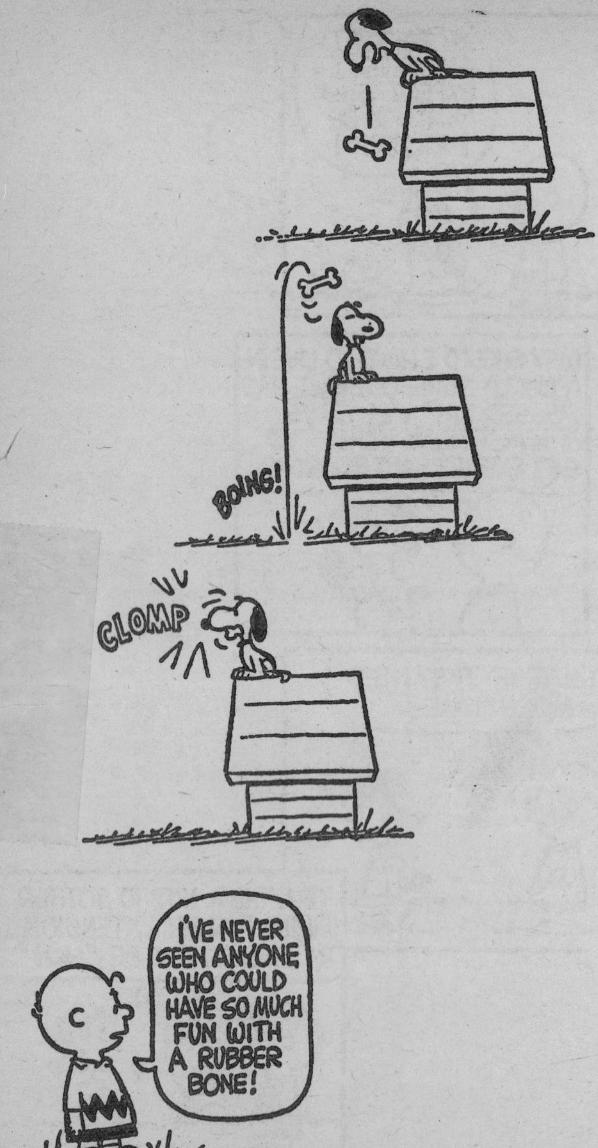
BOING!
CLOMP
I'VE NEVER SEEN ANYONE WHO COULD HAVE SO MUCH FUN WITH A RUBBER BONE!

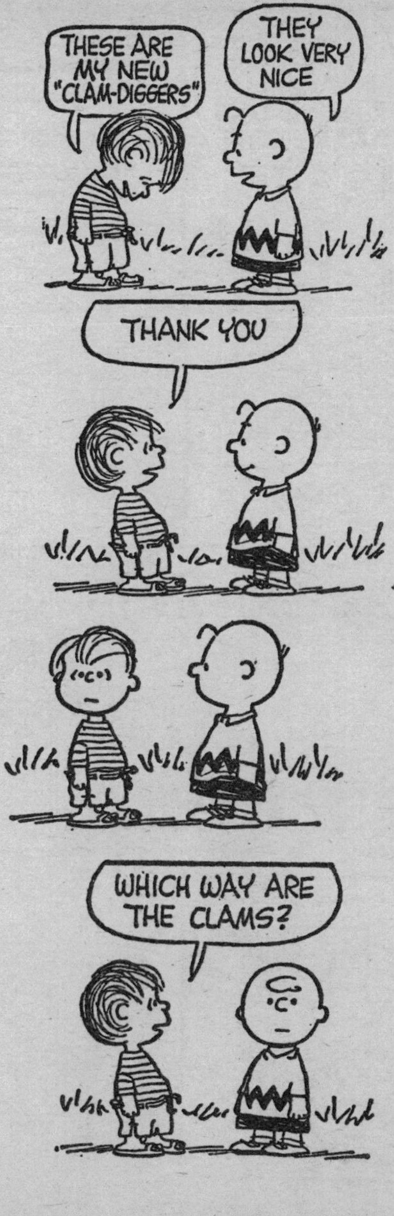
THESE ARE MY NEW "CLAM-DIGGERS"
THEY LOOK VERY NICE
THANK YOU
WHICH WAY ARE THE CLAMS?

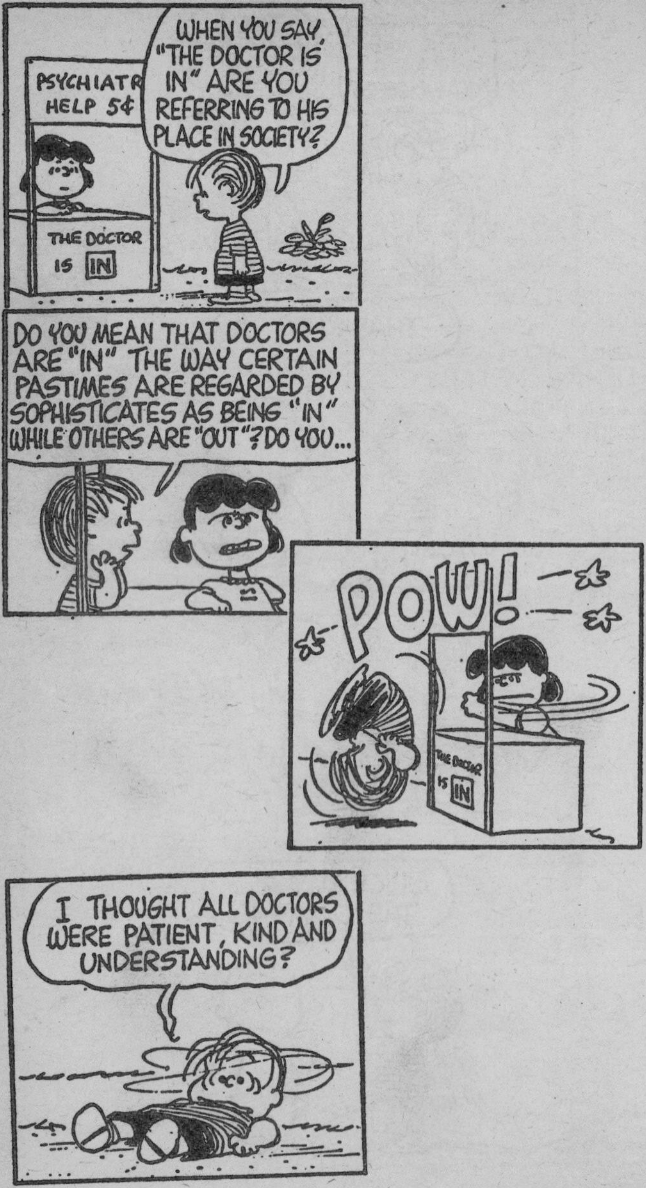

PSYCHIATR HELP 5¢
WHEN YOU SAY, "THE DOCTOR IS IN" ARE YOU REFERRING TO HIS PLACE IN SOCIETY?
THE DOCTOR IS IN
DO YOU MEAN THAT DOCTORS ARE "IN" THE WAY CERTAIN PASTIMES ARE REGARDED BY SOPHISTICATES AS BEING "IN" WHILE OTHERS ARE "OUT"? DO YOU...
POW!
THE DOCTOR IS IN
I THOUGHT ALL DOCTORS WERE PATIENT, KIND AND UNDERSTANDING?

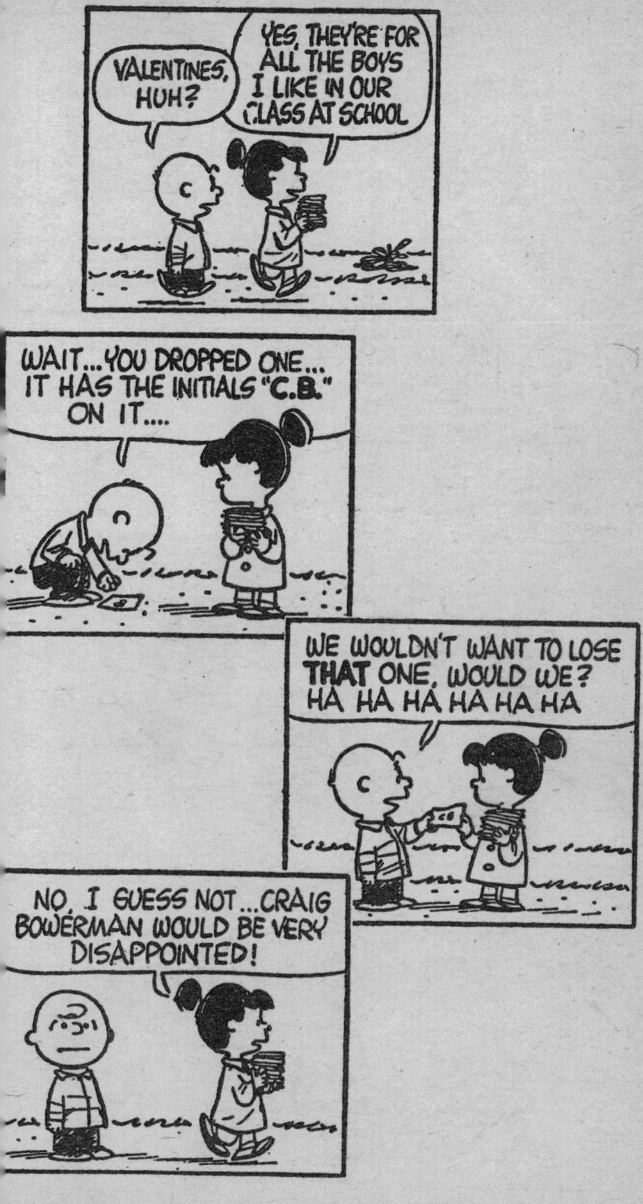

VALENTINES, HUH?
YES, THEY'RE FOR ALL THE BOYS I LIKE IN OUR CLASS AT SCHOOL
WAIT...YOU DROPPED ONE... IT HAS THE INITIALS "C.B." ON IT....
WE WOULDN'T WANT TO LOSE THAT ONE, WOULD WE? HA HA HA HA HA HA
NO, I GUESS NOT...CRAIG BOWERMAN WOULD BE VERY DISAPPOINTED!

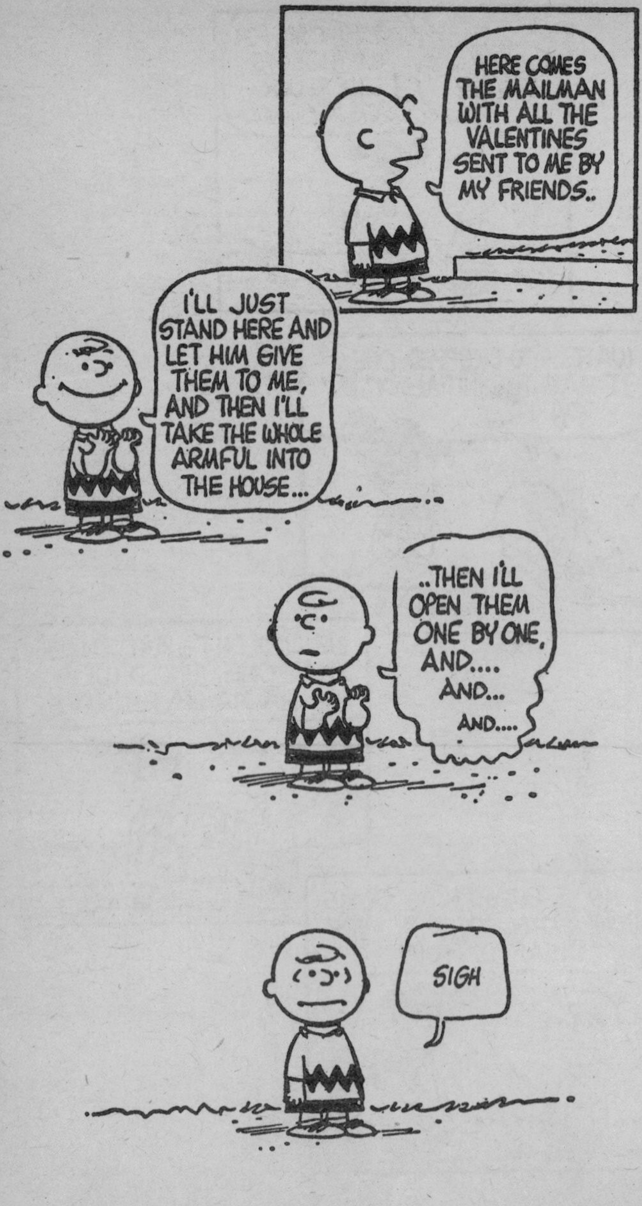
HERE COMES THE MAILMAN WITH ALL THE VALENTINES SENT TO ME BY MY FRIENDS..
I'LL JUST STAND HERE AND LET HIM GIVE THEM TO ME, AND THEN I'LL TAKE THE WHOLE ARMFUL INTO THE HOUSE...
..THEN I'LL OPEN THEM ONE BY ONE, AND.... AND... AND....
SIGH

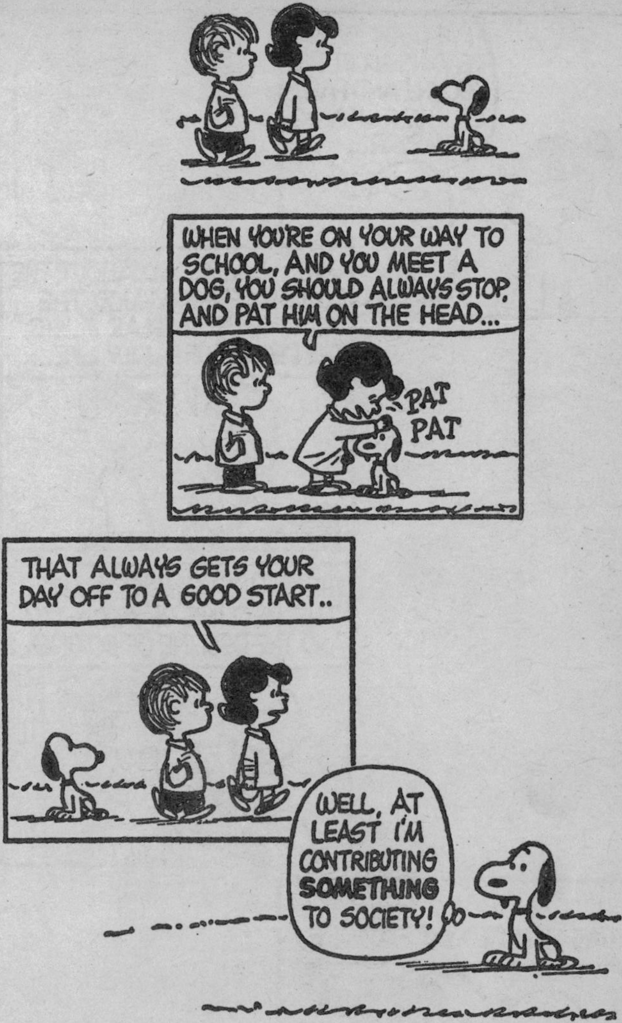
WHEN YOU'RE ON YOUR WAY TO SCHOOL, AND YOU MEET A DOG, YOU SHOULD ALWAYS STOP, AND PAT HIM ON THE HEAD...
PAT PAT
THAT ALWAYS GETS YOUR DAY OFF TO A GOOD START..
WELL, AT LEAST I'M CONTRIBUTING SOMETHING TO SOCIETY!

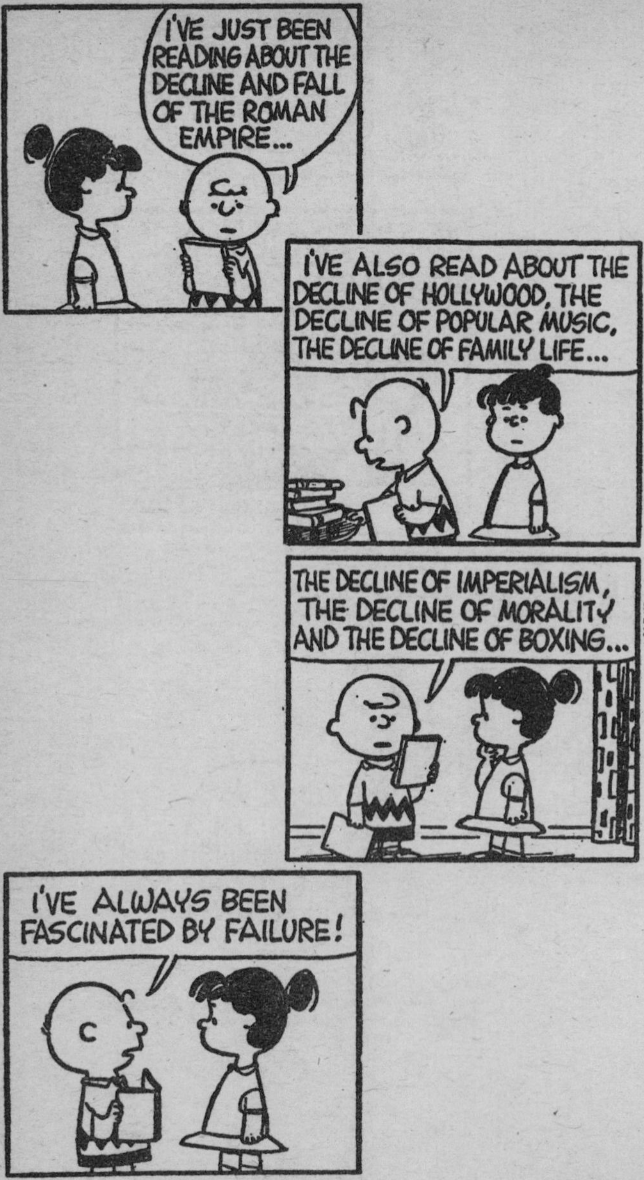
I'VE JUST BEEN READING ABOUT THE DECLINE AND FALL OF THE ROMAN EMPIRE...
I'VE ALSO READ ABOUT THE DECLINE OF HOLLYWOOD, THE DECLINE OF POPULAR MUSIC, THE DECLINE OF FAMILY LIFE...
THE DECLINE OF IMPERIALISM, THE DECLINE OF MORALITY AND THE DECLINE OF BOXING...
I'VE ALWAYS BEEN FASCINATED BY FAILURE!

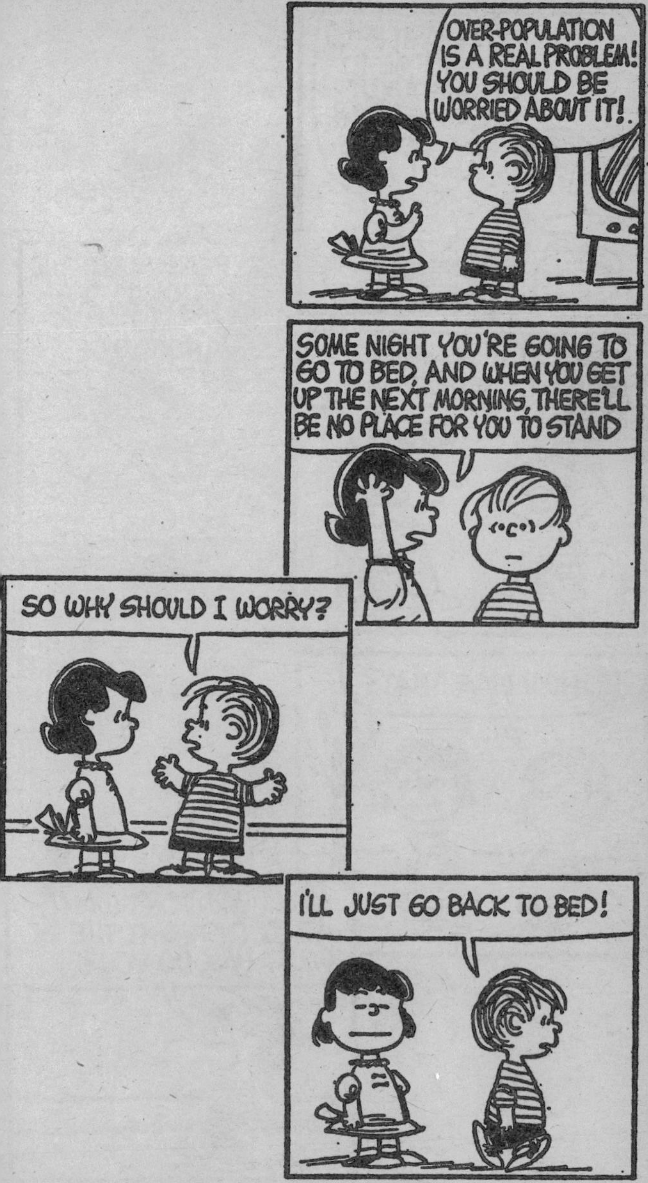
OVER-POPULATION IS A REAL PROBLEM! YOU SHOULD BE WORRIED ABOUT IT!
SOME NIGHT YOU'RE GOING TO GO TO BED, AND WHEN YOU GET UP THE NEXT MORNING, THERE'LL BE NO PLACE FOR YOU TO STAND
SO WHY SHOULD I WORRY?
I'LL JUST GO BACK TO BED!

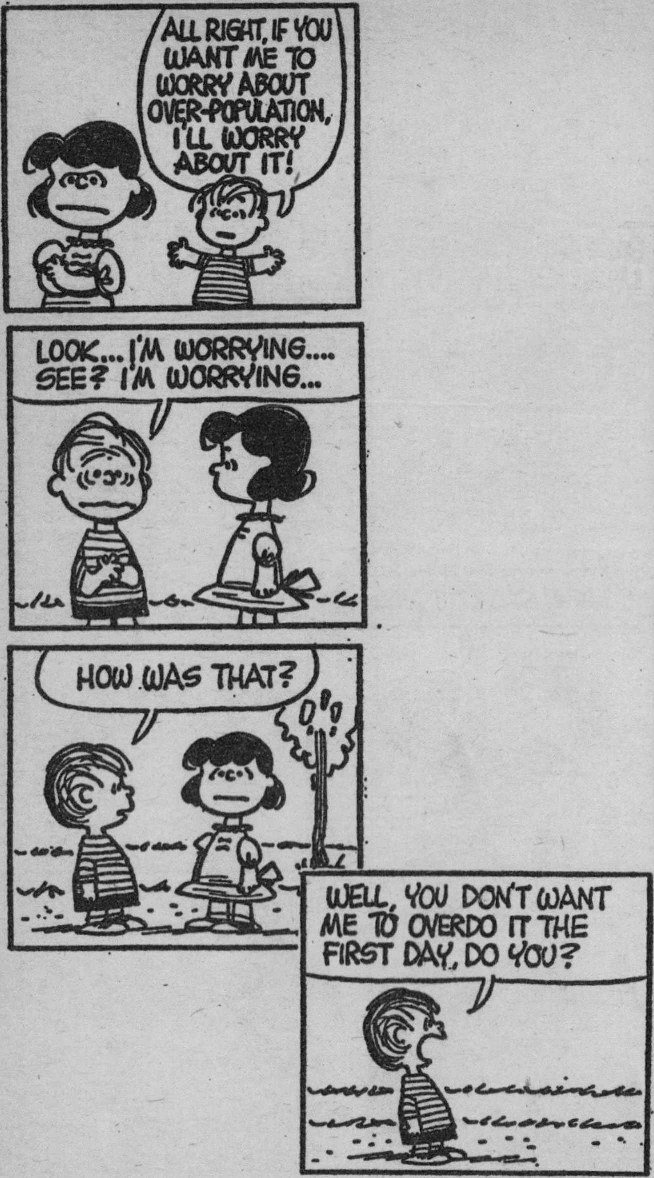
ALL RIGHT, IF YOU WANT ME TO WORRY ABOUT OVER-POPULATION, I'LL WORRY ABOUT IT!
LOOK... I'M WORRYING.... SEE? I'M WORRYING...
HOW WAS THAT?
WELL, YOU DON'T WANT ME TO OVERDO IT THE FIRST DAY, DO YOU?

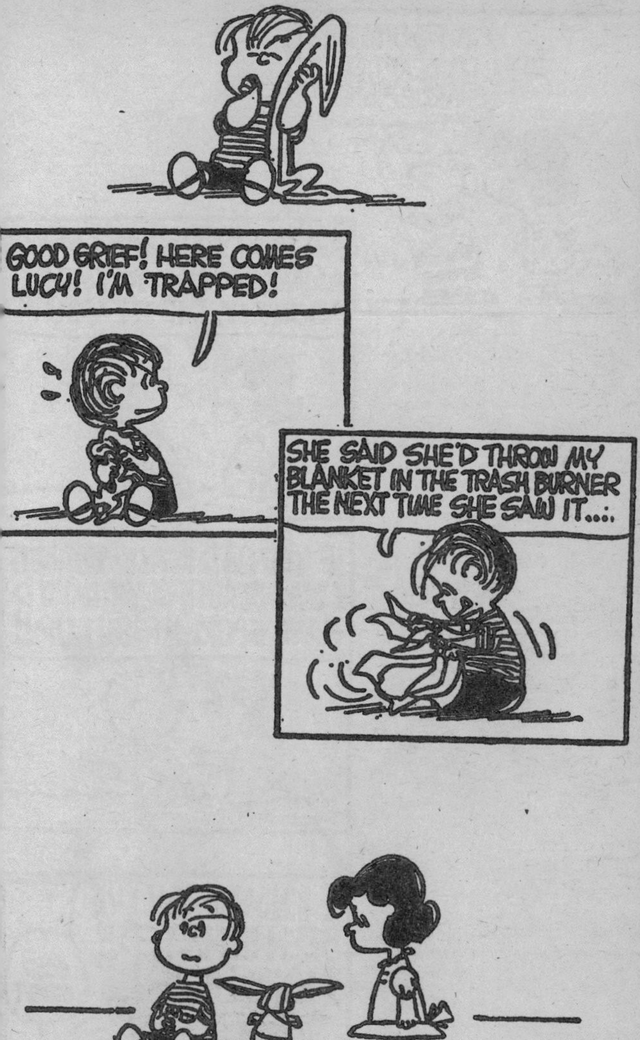
GOOD GRIEF! HERE COMES LUCY! I'M TRAPPED!
SHE SAID SHE'D THROW MY BLANKET IN THE TRASH BURNER THE NEXT TIME SHE SAW IT...

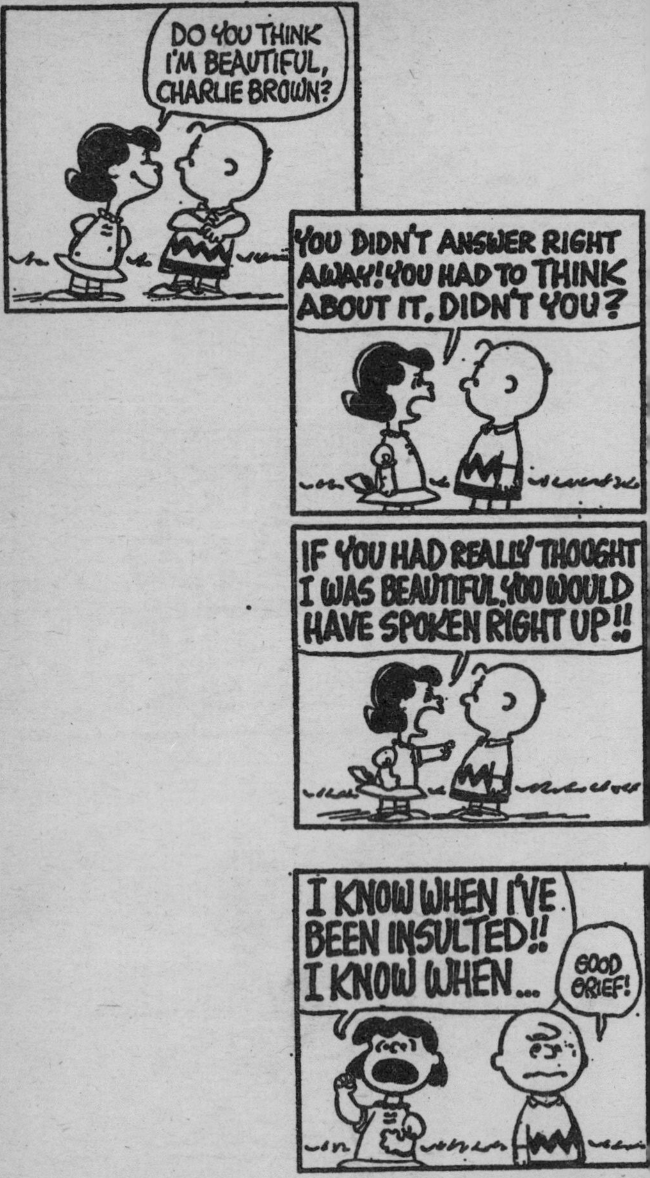
DO YOU THINK I'M BEAUTIFUL, CHARLIE BROWN?
YOU DIDN'T ANSWER RIGHT AWAY! YOU HAD TO THINK ABOUT IT, DIDN'T YOU?
IF YOU HAD REALLY THOUGHT I WAS BEAUTIFUL, YOU WOULD HAVE SPOKEN RIGHT UP!!
I KNOW WHEN I'VE BEEN INSULTED!! I KNOW WHEN...
GOOD GRIEF!

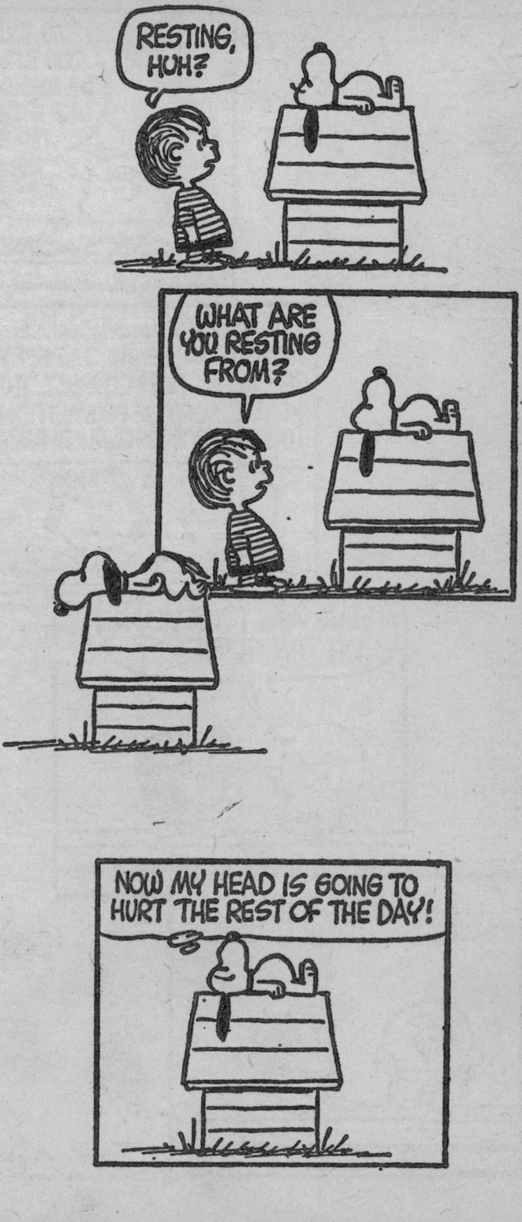
RESTING, HUH?
WHAT ARE YOU RESTING FROM?
NOW MY HEAD IS GOING TO HURT THE REST OF THE DAY!

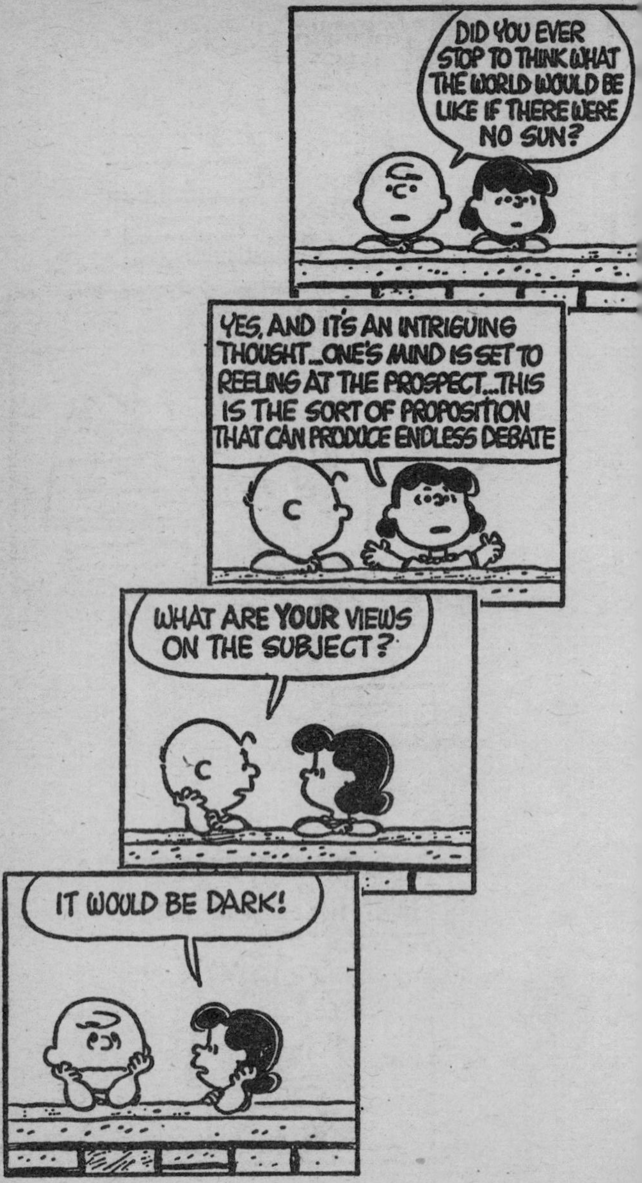
DID YOU EVER STOP TO THINK WHAT THE WORLD WOULD BE LIKE IF THERE WERE NO SUN?
YES, AND IT'S AN INTRIGUING THOUGHT...ONE'S MIND IS SET TO REELING AT THE PROSPECT...THIS IS THE SORT OF PROPOSITION THAT CAN PRODUCE ENDLESS DEBATE
WHAT ARE YOUR VIEWS ON THE SUBJECT?
IT WOULD BE DARK!

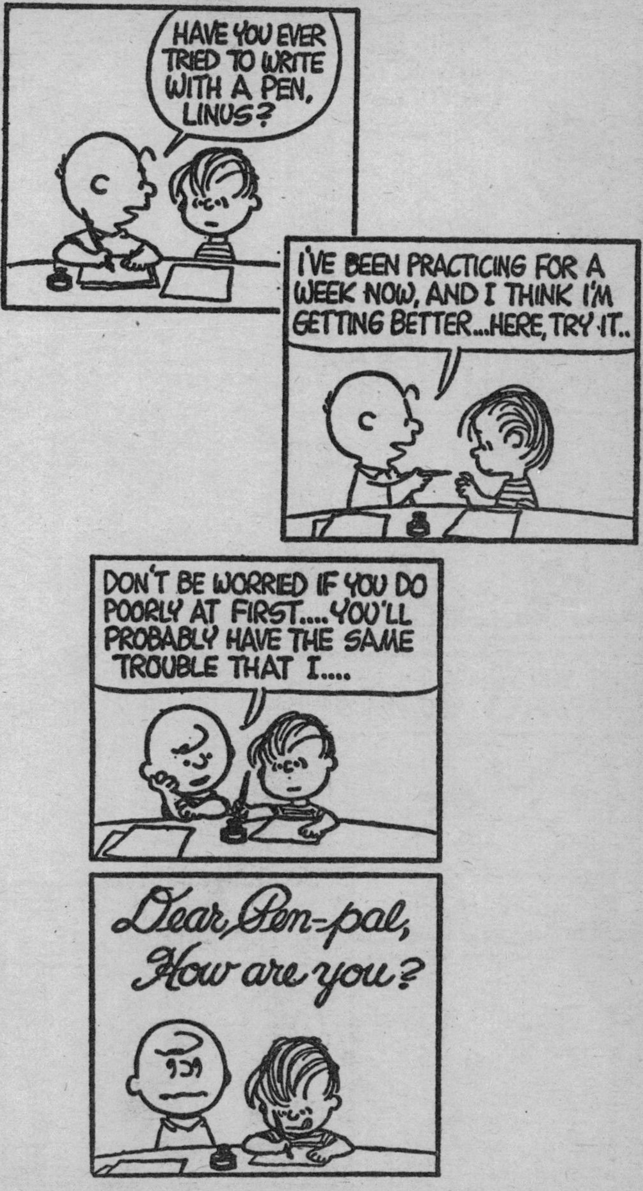
HAVE YOU EVER TRIED TO WRITE WITH A PEN, LINUS?
I'VE BEEN PRACTICING FOR A WEEK NOW, AND I THINK I'M GETTING BETTER...HERE, TRY IT..
DON'T BE WORRIED IF YOU DO POORLY AT FIRST....YOU'LL PROBABLY HAVE THE SAME TROUBLE THAT I....
Dear Pen-pal,
How are you?

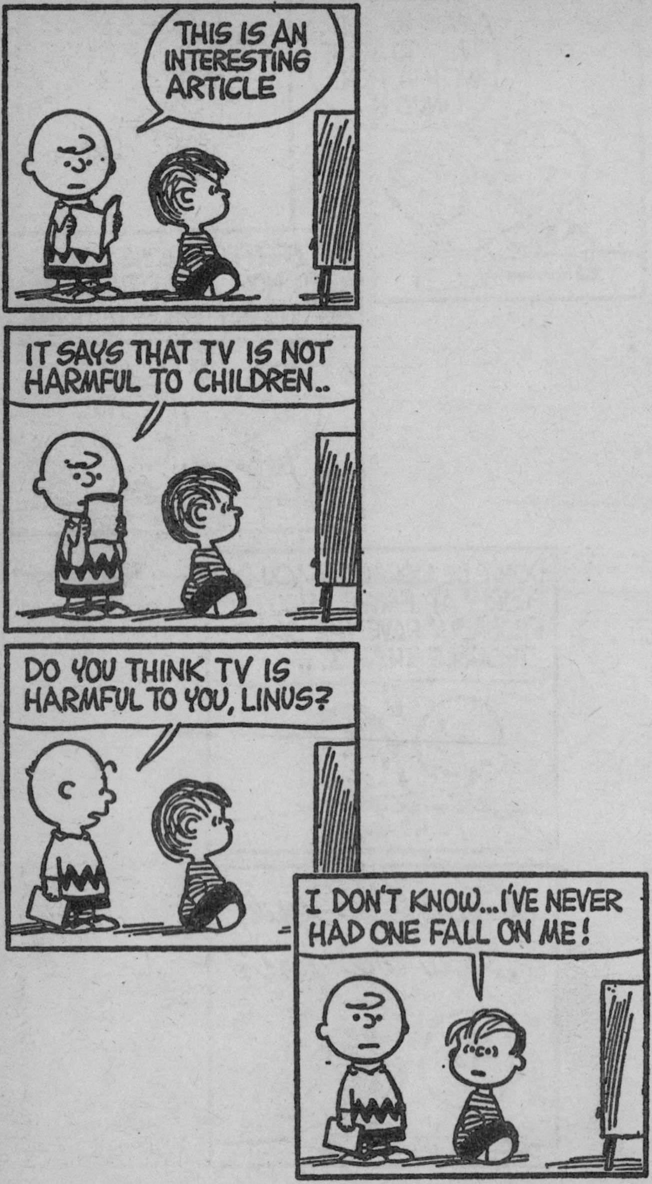
THIS IS AN INTERESTING ARTICLE
IT SAYS THAT TV IS NOT HARMFUL TO CHILDREN..
DO YOU THINK TV IS HARMFUL TO YOU, LINUS?
I DON'T KNOW...I'VE NEVER HAD ONE FALL ON ME!

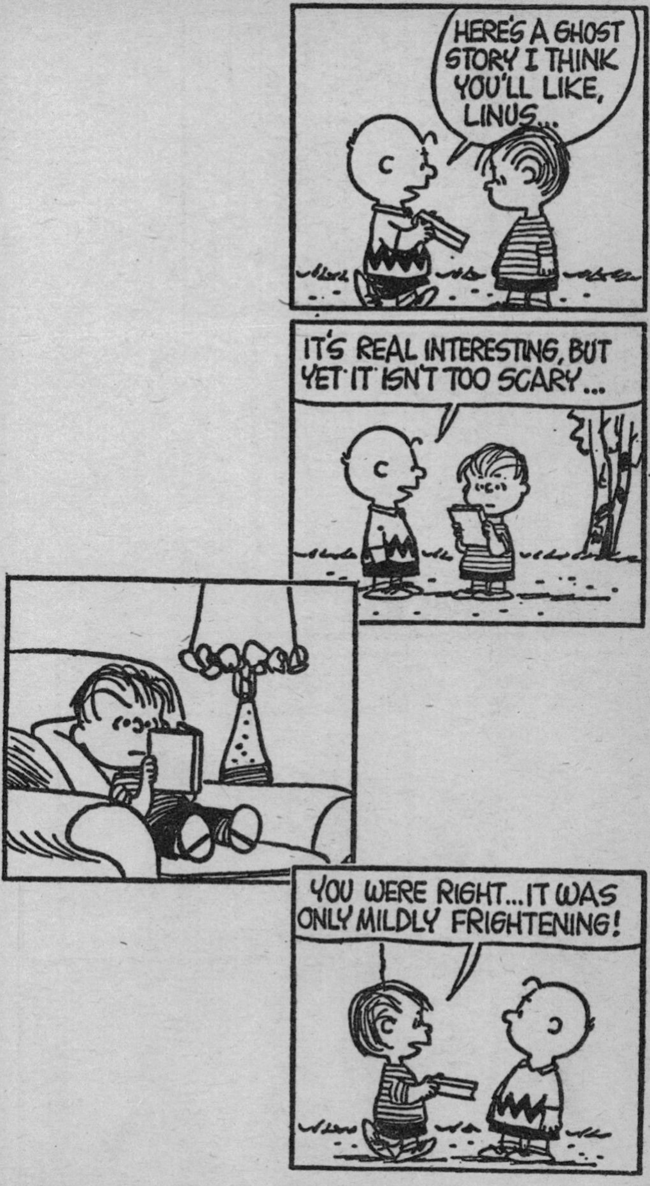
HERE'S A GHOST STORY I THINK YOU'LL LIKE, LINUS...
IT'S REAL INTERESTING, BUT YET IT ISN'T TOO SCARY...
YOU WERE RIGHT...IT WAS ONLY MILDLY FRIGHTENING!

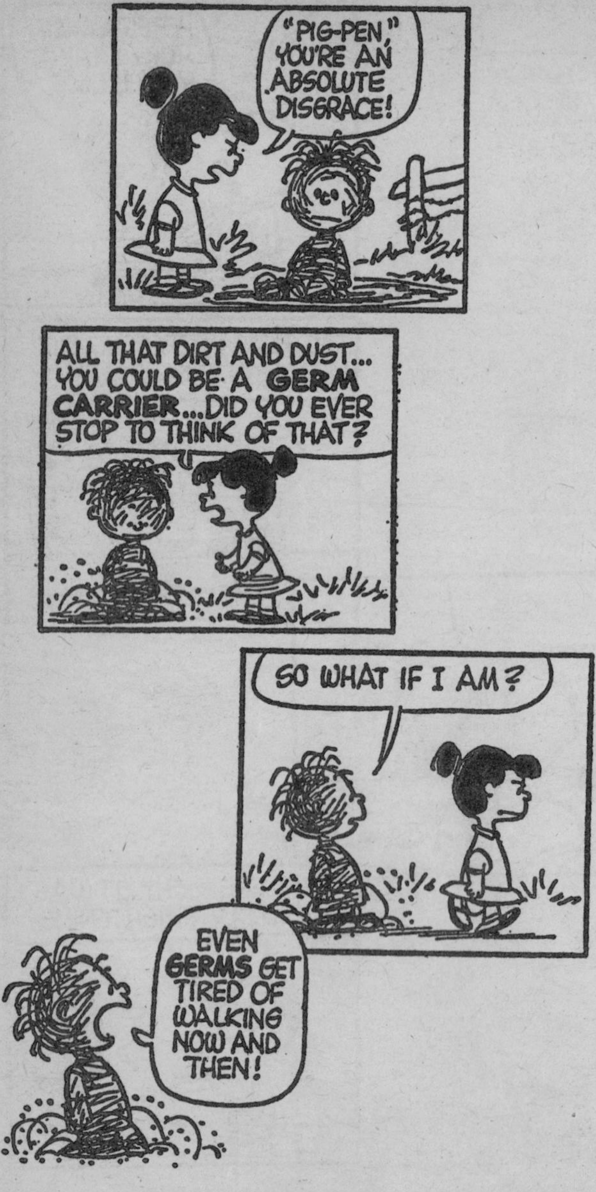
"PIG-PEN," YOU'RE AN ABSOLUTE DISGRACE!
ALL THAT DIRT AND DUST... YOU COULD BE A GERM CARRIER...DID YOU EVER STOP TO THINK OF THAT?
SO WHAT IF I AM?
EVEN GERMS GET TIRED OF WALKING NOW AND THEN!

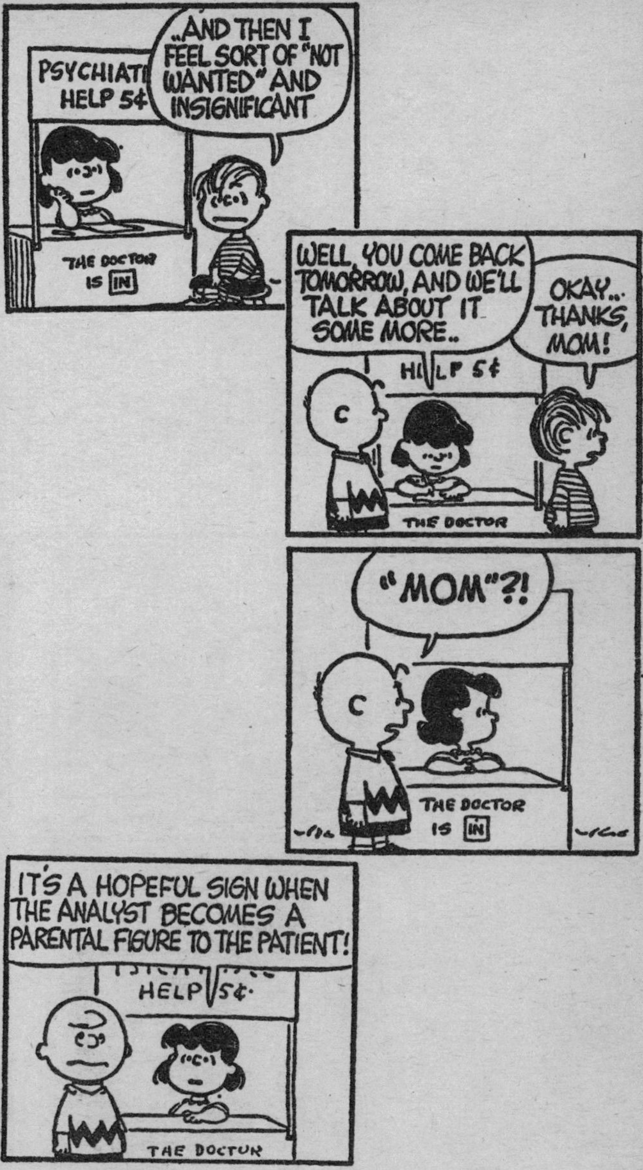
PSYCHIATI
HELP 5¢
..AND THEN I FEEL SORT OF "NOT WANTED" AND INSIGNIFICANT
THE DOCTOR IS IN
WELL, YOU COME BACK TOMORROW, AND WE'LL TALK ABOUT IT SOME MORE..
OKAY... THANKS, MOM!
HELP 5¢
THE DOCTOR
"MOM"?!
THE DOCTOR IS IN
IT'S A HOPEFUL SIGN WHEN THE ANALYST BECOMES A PARENTAL FIGURE TO THE PATIENT!
HELP 5¢
THE DOCTOR

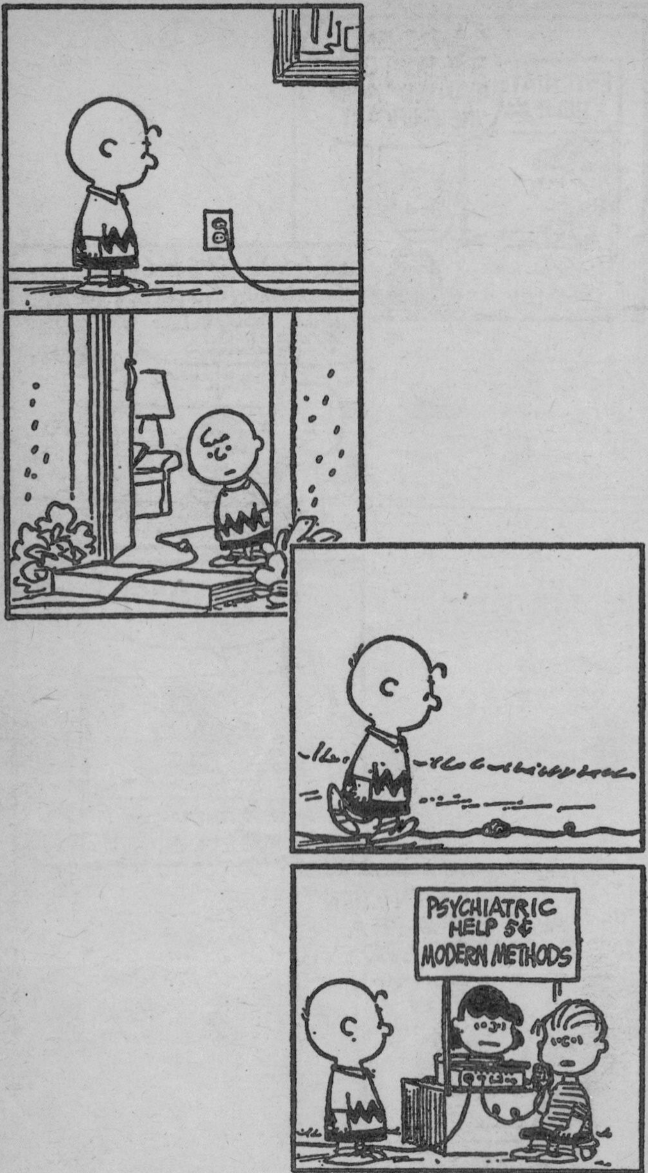
PSYCHIATRIC
HELP 5¢
MODERN METHODS

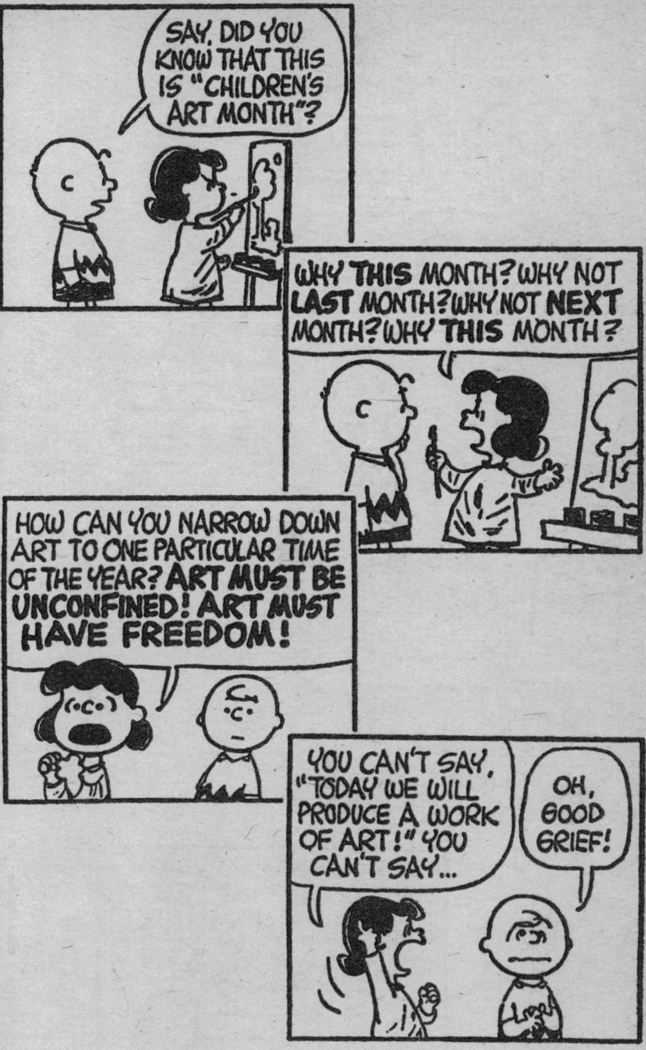
SAY, DID YOU KNOW THAT THIS IS "CHILDREN'S ART MONTH"?
WHY THIS MONTH? WHY NOT LAST MONTH? WHY NOT NEXT MONTH? WHY THIS MONTH?
HOW CAN YOU NARROW DOWN ART TO ONE PARTICULAR TIME OF THE YEAR? ART MUST BE UNCONFINED! ART MUST HAVE FREEDOM!
YOU CAN'T SAY, "TODAY WE WILL PRODUCE A WORK OF ART!" YOU CAN'T SAY...
OH, GOOD GRIEF!

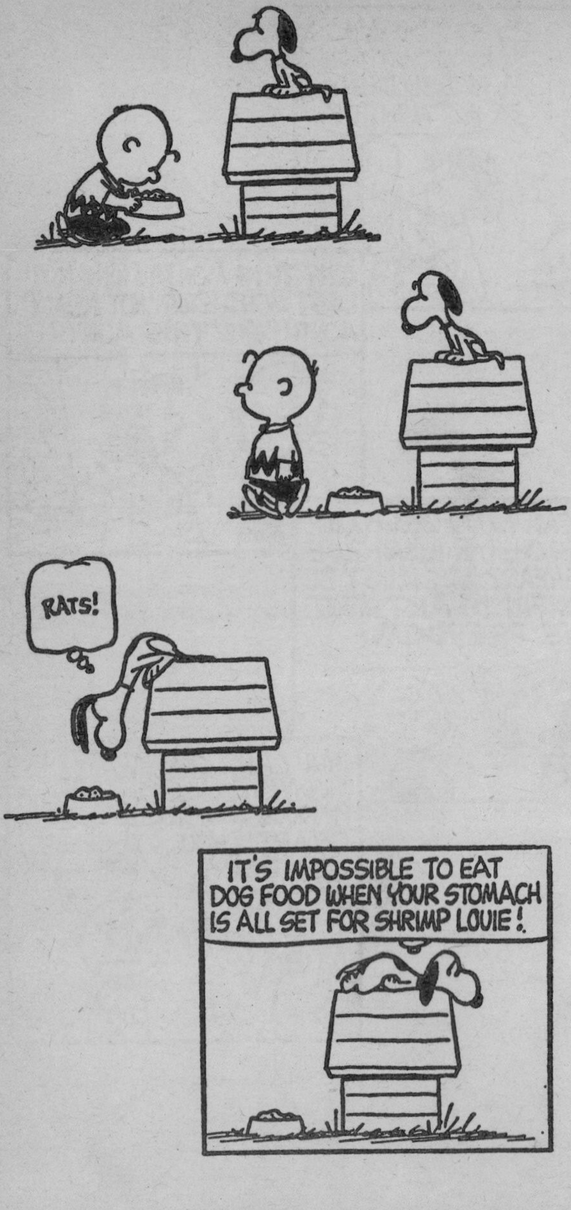
RATS!
IT'S IMPOSSIBLE TO EAT DOG FOOD WHEN YOUR STOMACH IS ALL SET FOR SHRIMP LOUIE!

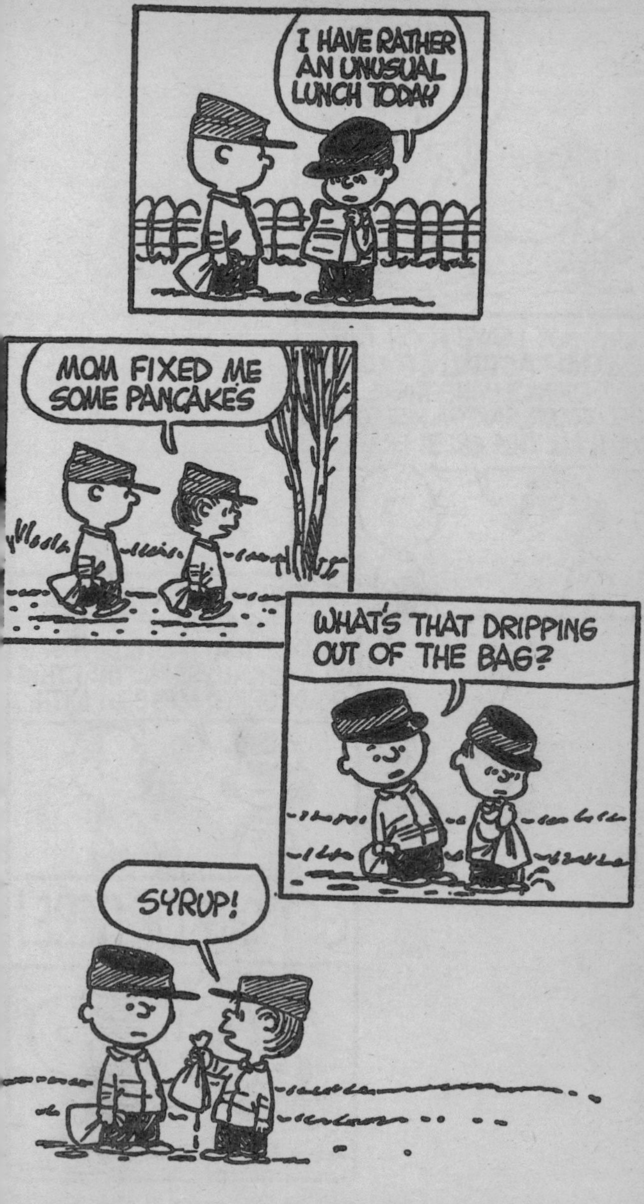
I HAVE RATHER AN UNUSUAL LUNCH TODAY
MOM FIXED ME SOME PANCAKES
WHAT'S THAT DRIPPING OUT OF THE BAG?
SYRUP!

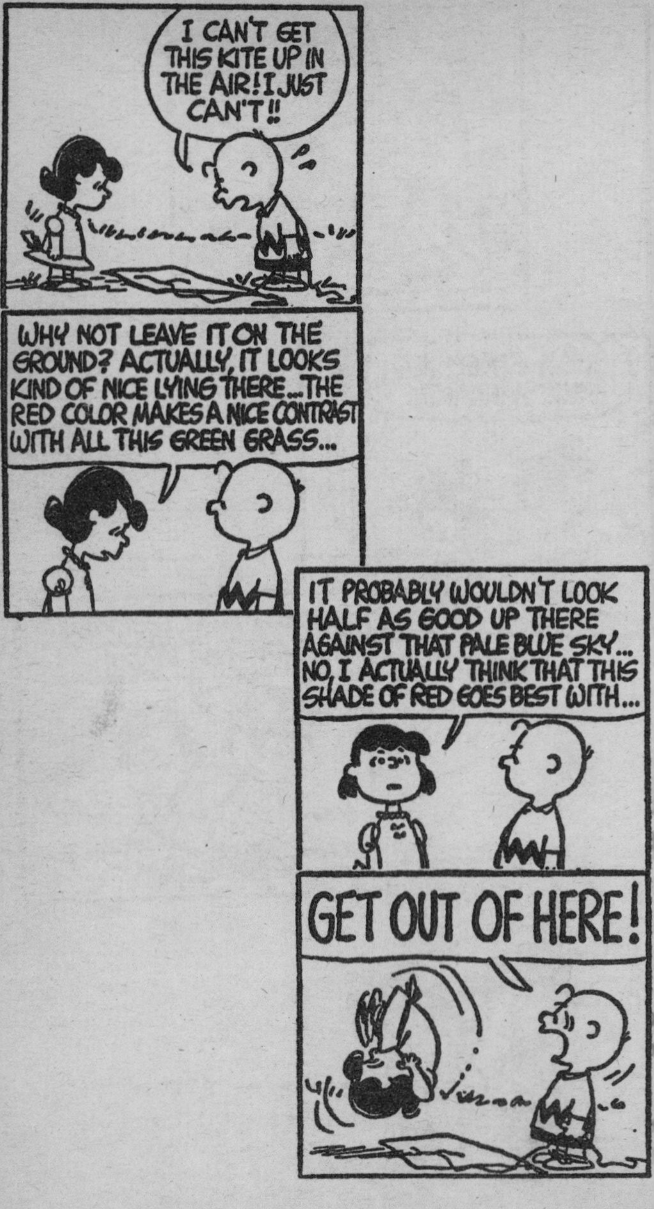

I CAN'T GET THIS KITE UP IN THE AIR! I JUST CAN'T!!
WHY NOT LEAVE IT ON THE GROUND? ACTUALLY, IT LOOKS KIND OF NICE LYING THERE...THE RED COLOR MAKES A NICE CONTRAST WITH ALL THIS GREEN GRASS...
IT PROBABLY WOULDN'T LOOK HALF AS GOOD UP THERE AGAINST THAT PALE BLUE SKY... NO, I ACTUALLY THINK THAT THIS SHADE OF RED GOES BEST WITH...
GET OUT OF HERE!

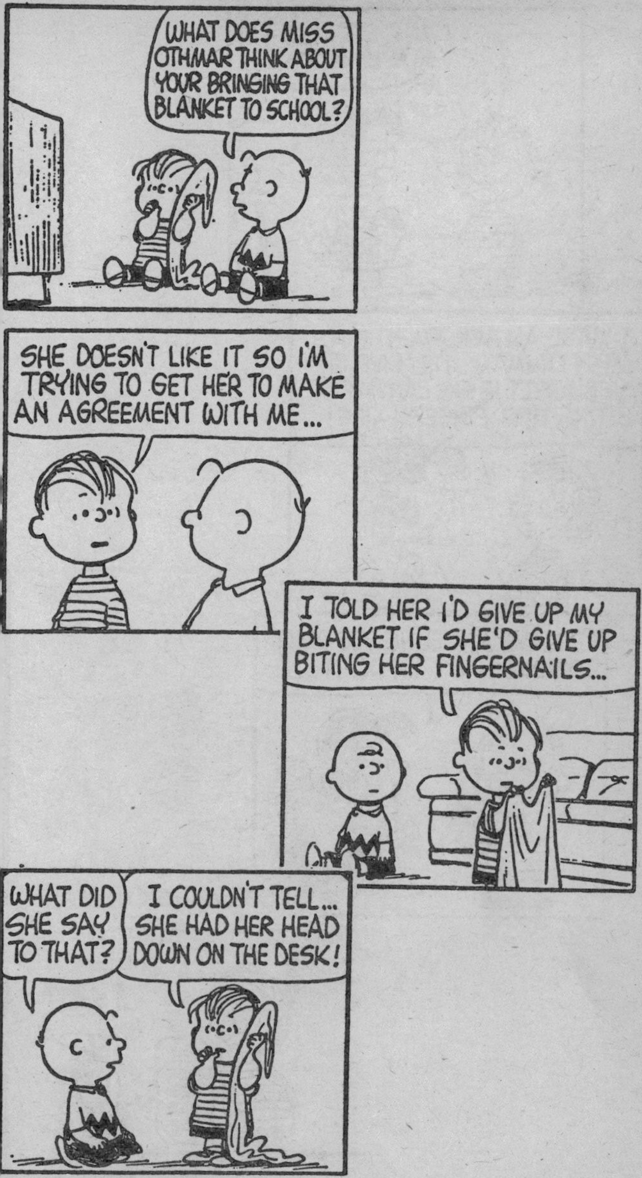
WHAT DOES MISS OTHMAR THINK ABOUT YOUR BRINGING THAT BLANKET TO SCHOOL?
SHE DOESN'T LIKE IT SO I'M TRYING TO GET HER TO MAKE AN AGREEMENT WITH ME...
I TOLD HER I'D GIVE UP MY BLANKET IF SHE'D GIVE UP BITING HER FINGERNAILS...
WHAT DID SHE SAY TO THAT?
I COULDN'T TELL... SHE HAD HER HEAD DOWN ON THE DESK!

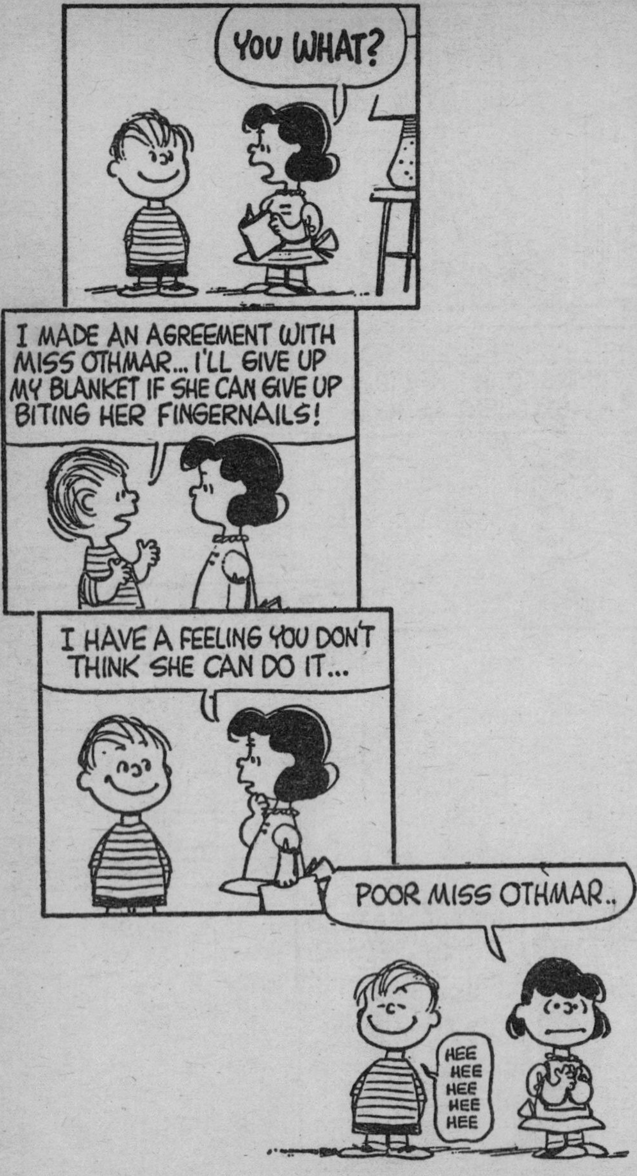
YOU WHAT?
I MADE AN AGREEMENT WITH MISS OTHMAR... I'LL GIVE UP MY BLANKET IF SHE CAN GIVE UP BITING HER FINGERNAILS!
I HAVE A FEELING YOU DON'T THINK SHE CAN DO IT...
POOR MISS OTHMAR..
HEE HEE HEE HEE HEE

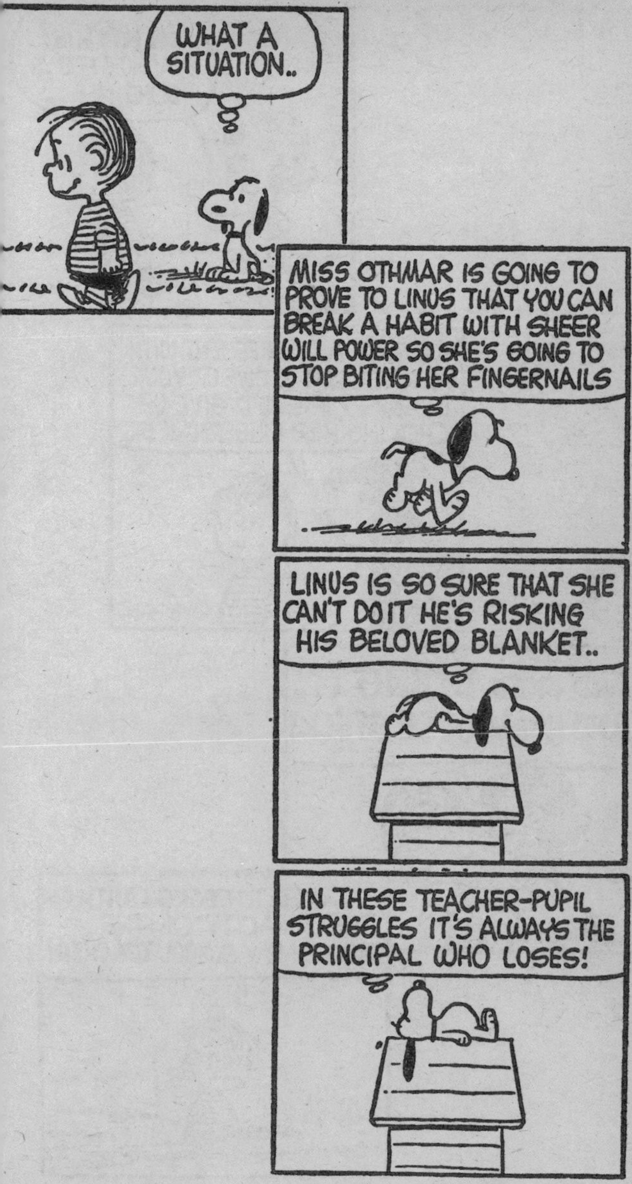
WHAT A SITUATION..
MISS OTHMAR IS GOING TO PROVE TO LINUS THAT YOU CAN BREAK A HABIT WITH SHEER WILL POWER SO SHE'S GOING TO STOP BITING HER FINGERNAILS
LINUS IS SO SURE THAT SHE CAN'T DO IT HE'S RISKING HIS BELOVED BLANKET..
IN THESE TEACHER-PUPIL STRUGGLES IT'S ALWAYS THE PRINCIPAL WHO LOSES!

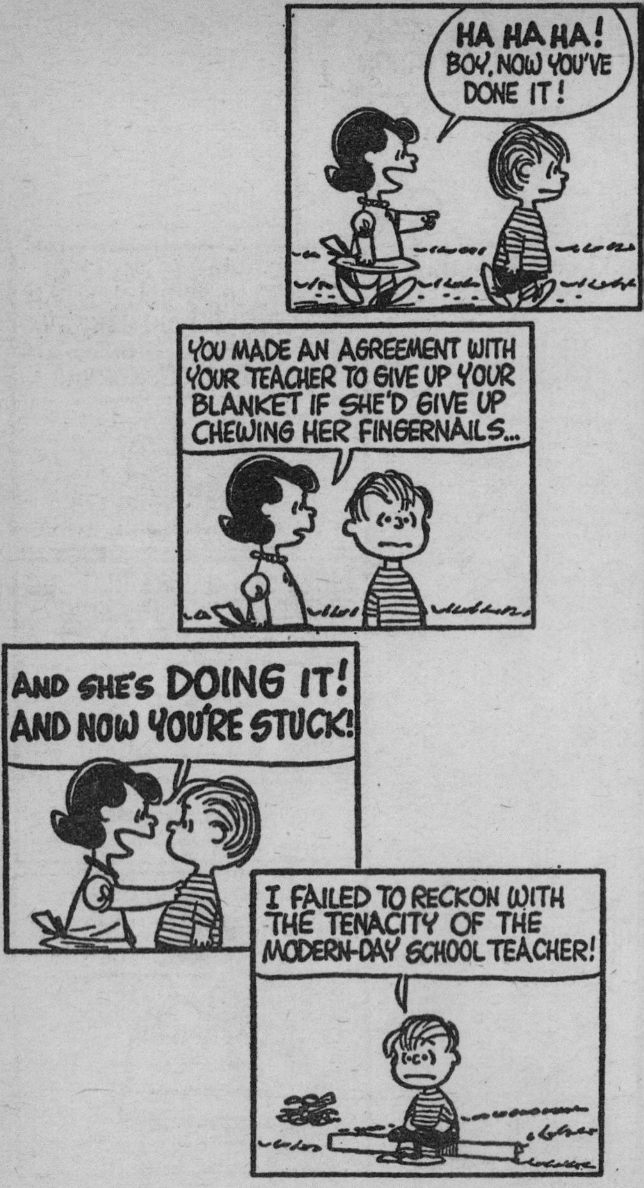
HA HA HA! BOY, NOW YOU'VE DONE IT!
YOU MADE AN AGREEMENT WITH YOUR TEACHER TO GIVE UP YOUR BLANKET IF SHE'D GIVE UP CHEWING HER FINGERNAILS...
AND SHE'S DOING IT! AND NOW YOU'RE STUCK!
I FAILED TO RECKON WITH THE TENACITY OF THE MODERN-DAY SCHOOL TEACHER!

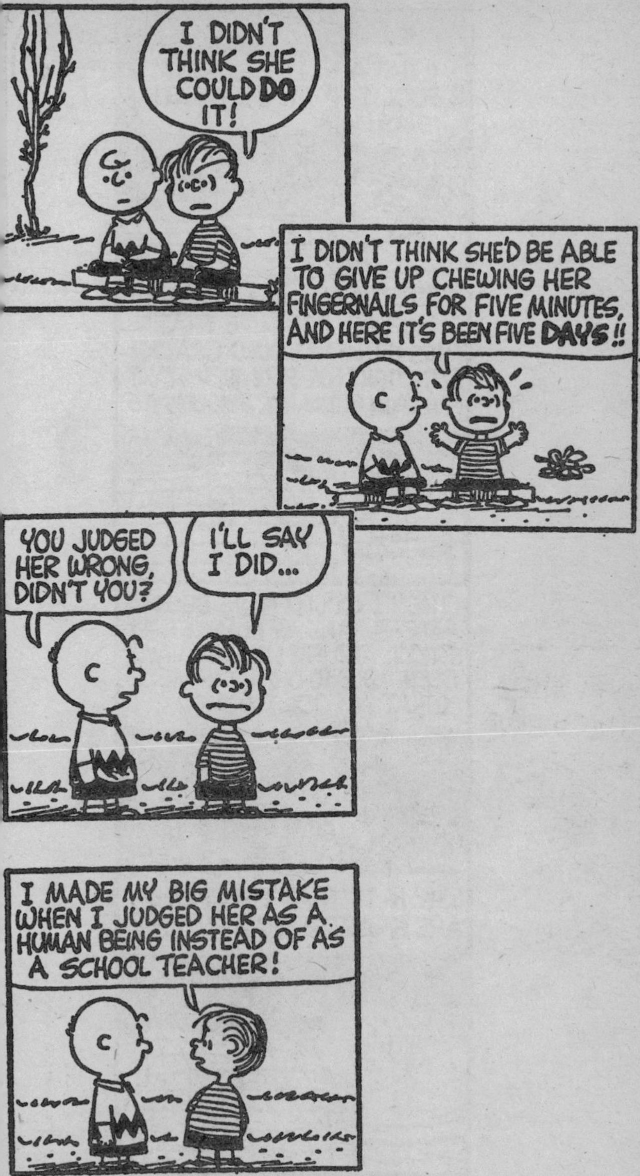
I DIDN'T THINK SHE COULD DO IT!
I DIDN'T THINK SHE'D BE ABLE TO GIVE UP CHEWING HER FINGERNAILS FOR FIVE MINUTES, AND HERE IT'S BEEN FIVE DAYS!!
YOU JUDGED HER WRONG, DIDN'T YOU?
I'LL SAY I DID...
I MADE MY BIG MISTAKE WHEN I JUDGED HER AS A HUMAN BEING INSTEAD OF AS A SCHOOL TEACHER!

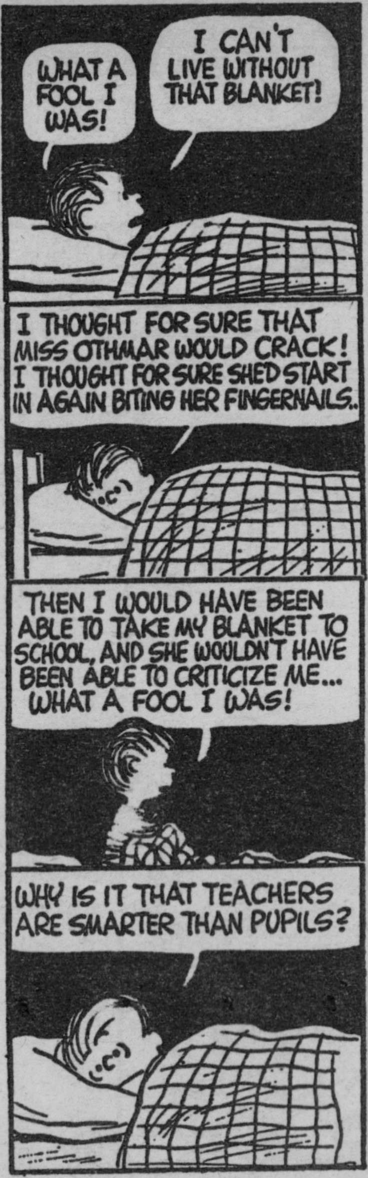
WHAT A FOOL I WAS!
I CAN'T LIVE WITHOUT THAT BLANKET!
I THOUGHT FOR SURE THAT MISS OTHMAR WOULD CRACK! I THOUGHT FOR SURE SHE'D START IN AGAIN BITING HER FINGERNAILS..
THEN I WOULD HAVE BEEN ABLE TO TAKE MY BLANKET TO SCHOOL, AND SHE WOULDN'T HAVE BEEN ABLE TO CRITICIZE ME... WHAT A FOOL I WAS!
WHY IS IT THAT TEACHERS ARE SMARTER THAN PUPILS?

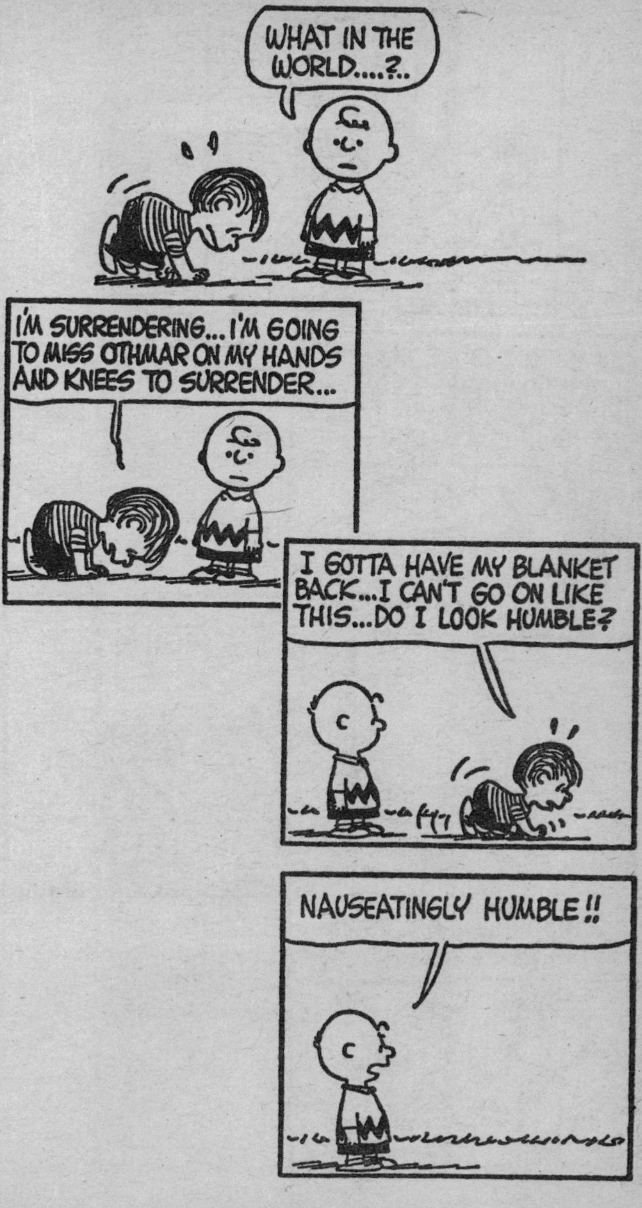
WHAT IN THE WORLD....?..
I'M SURRENDERING... I'M GOING TO MISS OTHMAR ON MY HANDS AND KNEES TO SURRENDER...
I GOTTA HAVE MY BLANKET BACK...I CAN'T GO ON LIKE THIS...DO I LOOK HUMBLE?
NAUSEATINGLY HUMBLE!!

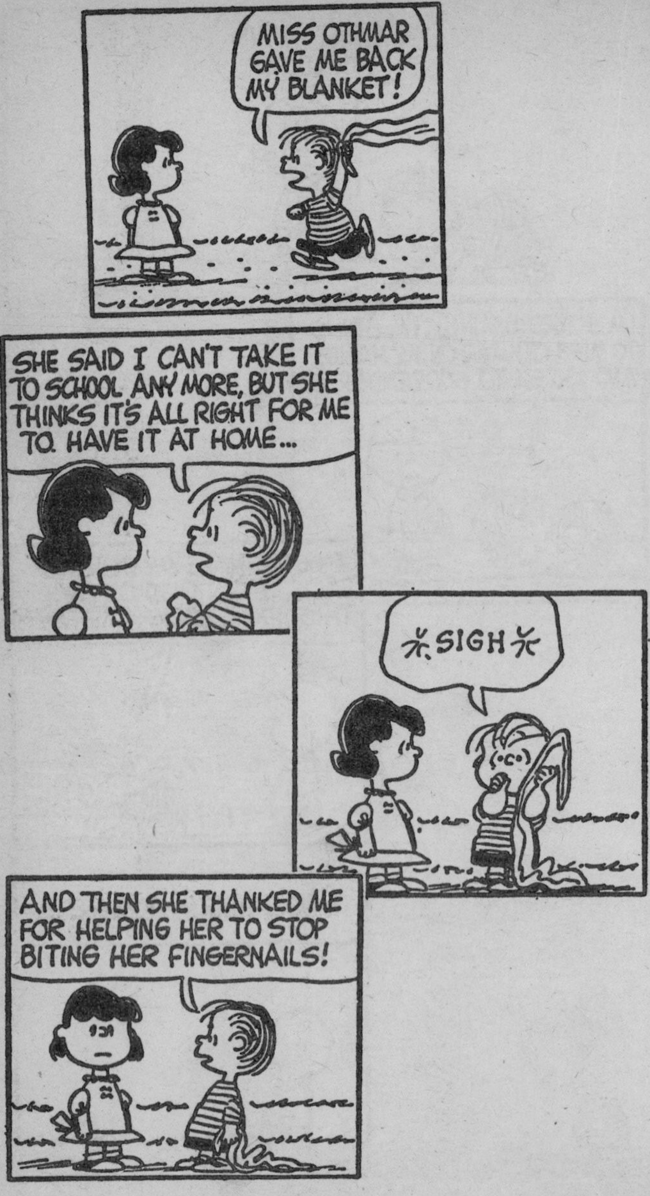
MISS OTHMAR GAVE ME BACK MY BLANKET!
SHE SAID I CAN'T TAKE IT TO SCHOOL ANY MORE, BUT SHE THINKS IT'S ALL RIGHT FOR ME TO HAVE IT AT HOME...
SIGH
AND THEN SHE THANKED ME FOR HELPING HER TO STOP BITING HER FINGERNAILS!

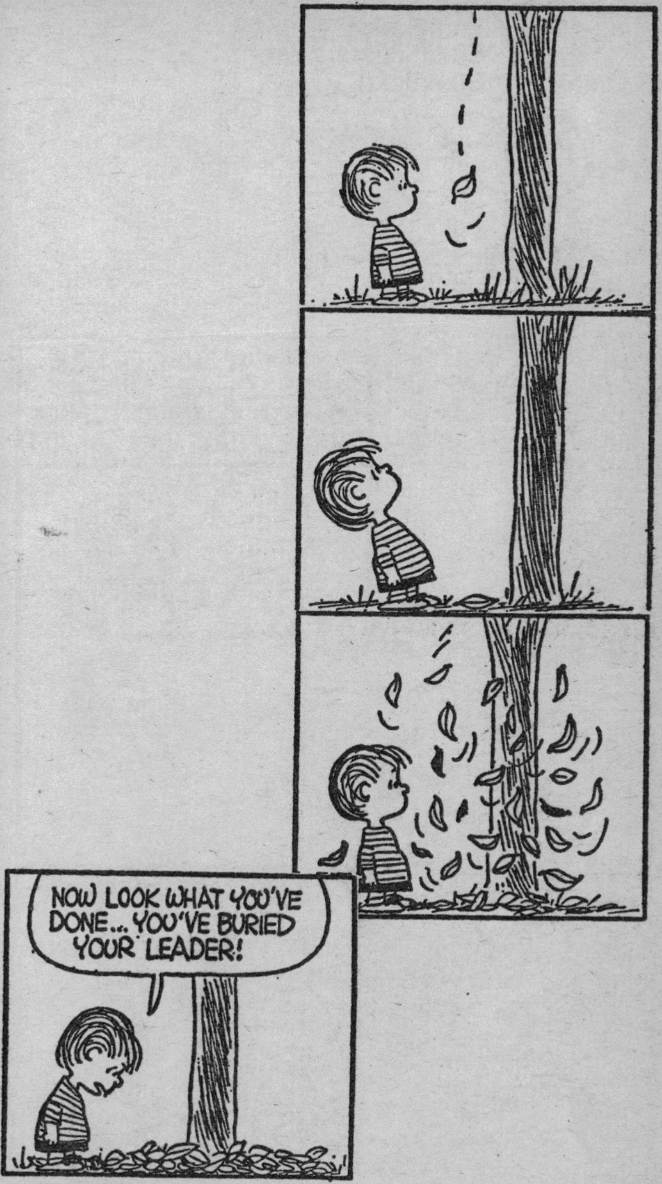
NOW LOOK WHAT YOU'VE DONE... YOU'VE BURIED YOUR LEADER!

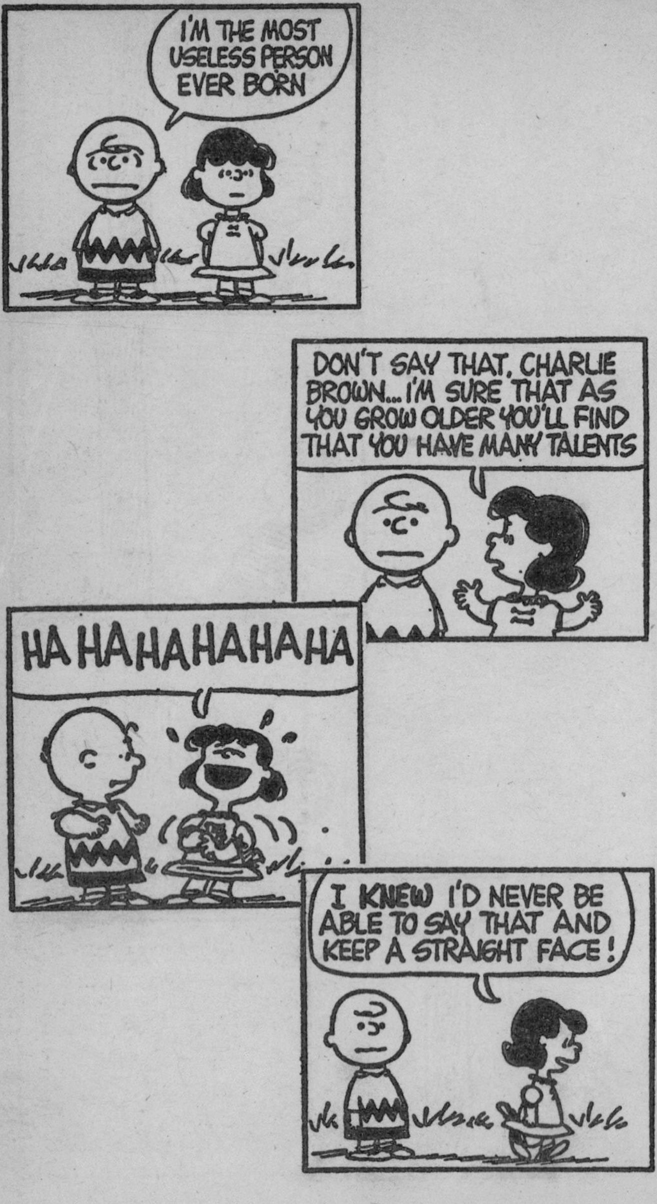
I'M THE MOST USELESS PERSON EVER BORN
DON'T SAY THAT, CHARLIE BROWN... I'M SURE THAT AS YOU GROW OLDER YOU'LL FIND THAT YOU HAVE MANY TALENTS
HA HA HA HA HA HA HA HA
I KNEW I'D NEVER BE ABLE TO SAY THAT AND KEEP A STRAIGHT FACE!

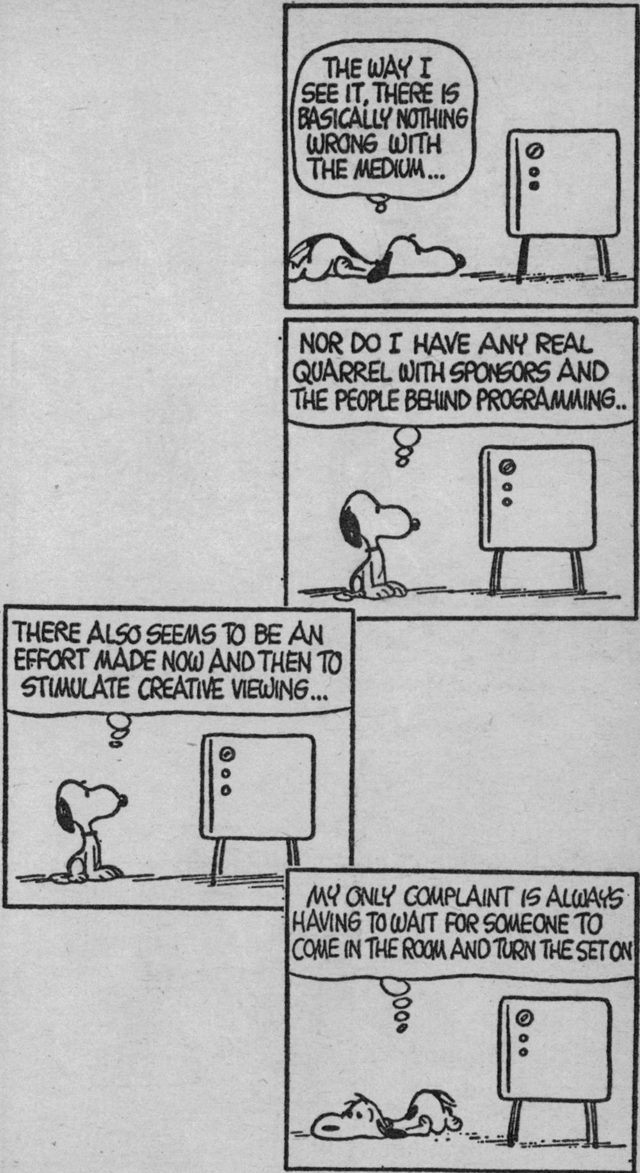

THE WAY I SEE IT, THERE IS BASICALLY NOTHING WRONG WITH THE MEDIUM...
NOR DO I HAVE ANY REAL QUARREL WITH SPONSORS AND THE PEOPLE BEHIND PROGRAMMING..
THERE ALSO SEEMS TO BE AN EFFORT MADE NOW AND THEN TO STIMULATE CREATIVE VIEWING...
MY ONLY COMPLAINT IS ALWAYS HAVING TO WAIT FOR SOMEONE TO COME IN THE ROOM AND TURN THE SET ON

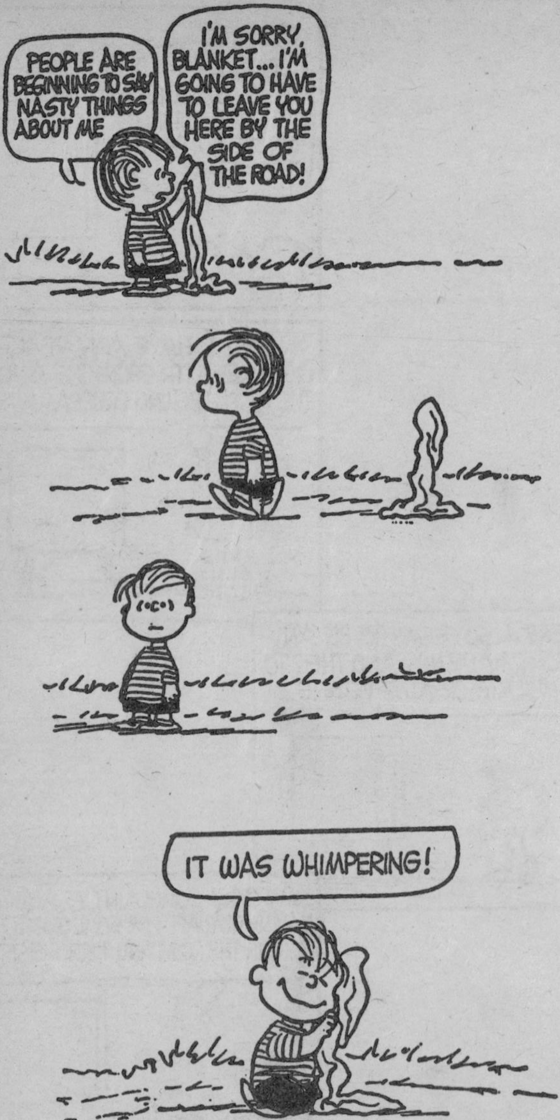
PEOPLE ARE BEGINNING TO SAY NASTY THINGS ABOUT ME
I'M SORRY, BLANKET... I'M GOING TO HAVE TO LEAVE YOU HERE BY THE SIDE OF THE ROAD!
IT WAS WHIMPERING!

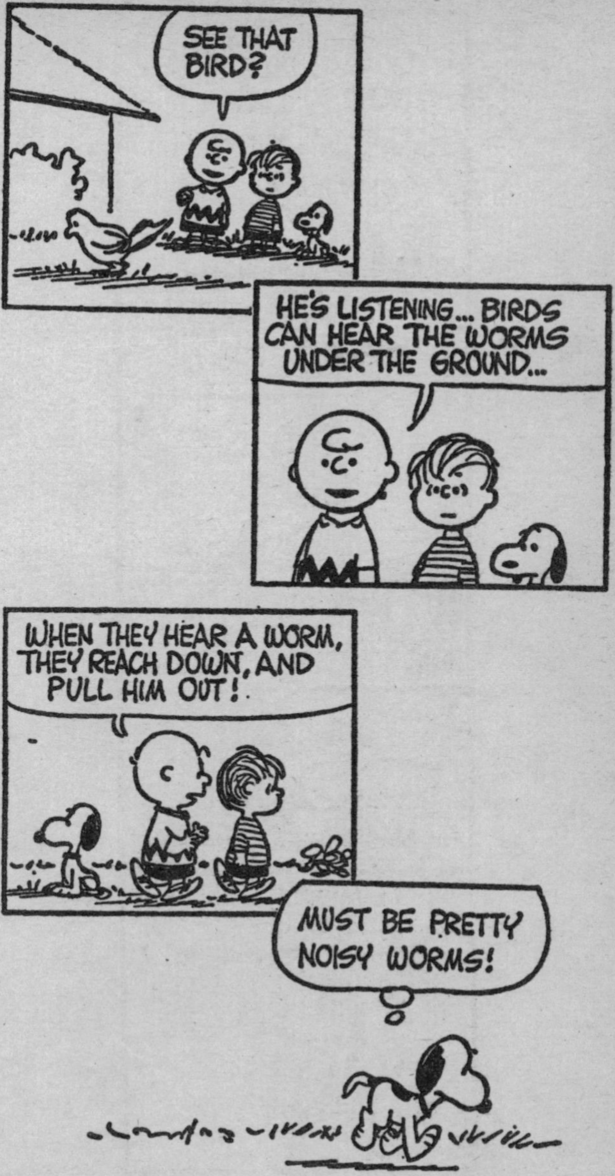
SEE THAT BIRD?
HE'S LISTENING... BIRDS CAN HEAR THE WORMS UNDER THE GROUND...
WHEN THEY HEAR A WORM, THEY REACH DOWN, AND PULL HIM OUT!
MUST BE PRETTY NOISY WORMS!

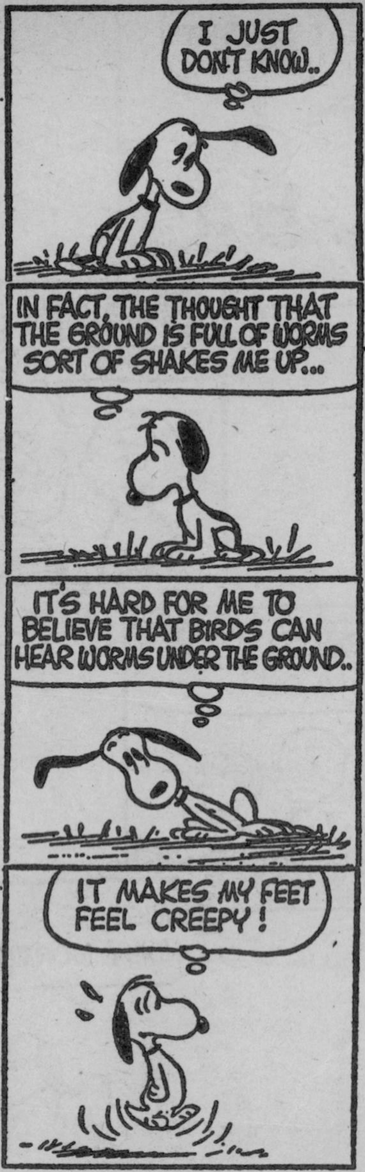
I JUST DON'T KNOW..
IN FACT, THE THOUGHT THAT THE GROUND IS FULL OF WORMS SORT OF SHAKES ME UP...
IT'S HARD FOR ME TO BELIEVE THAT BIRDS CAN HEAR WORMS UNDER THE GROUND..
IT MAKES MY FEET FEEL CREEPY!

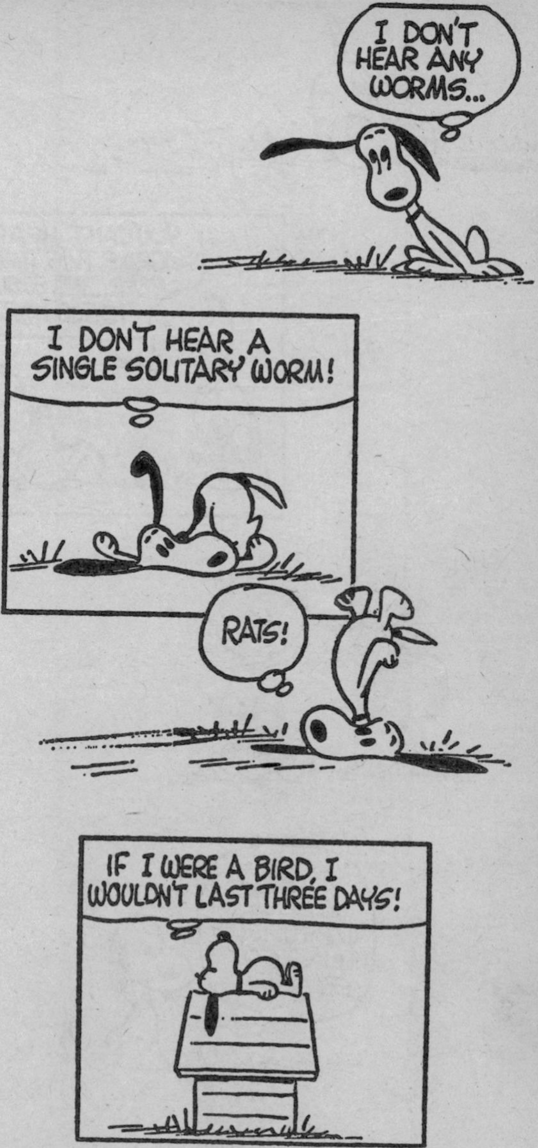
I DON'T HEAR ANY WORMS...
I DON'T HEAR A SINGLE SOLITARY WORM!
RATS!
IF I WERE A BIRD, I WOULDN'T LAST THREE DAYS!

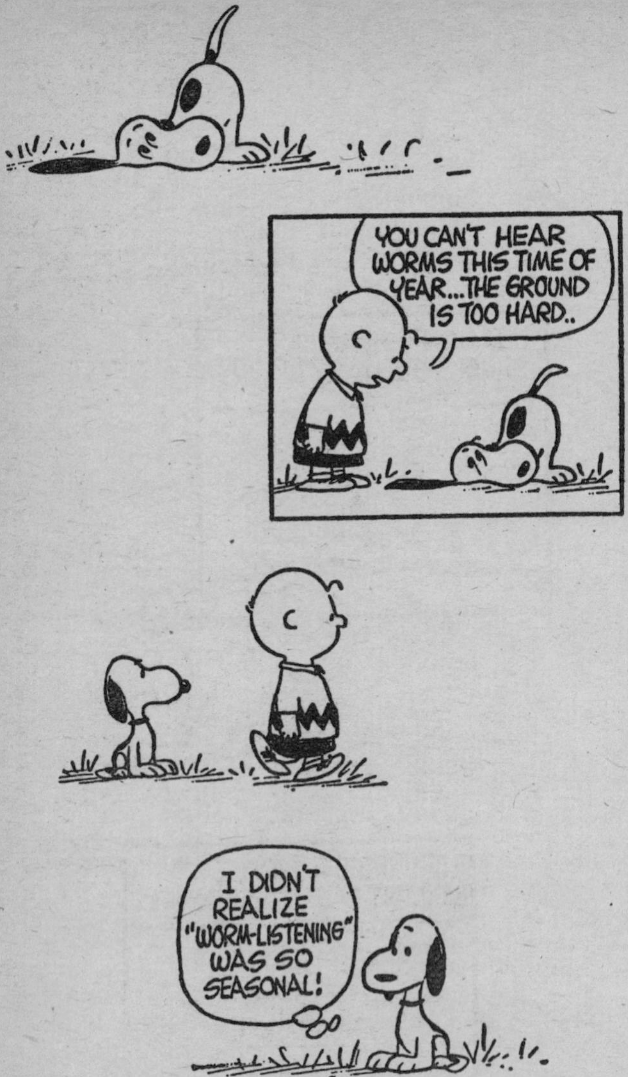
YOU CAN'T HEAR WORMS THIS TIME OF YEAR...THE GROUND IS TOO HARD..
I DIDN'T REALIZE "WORM-LISTENING" WAS SO SEASONAL!

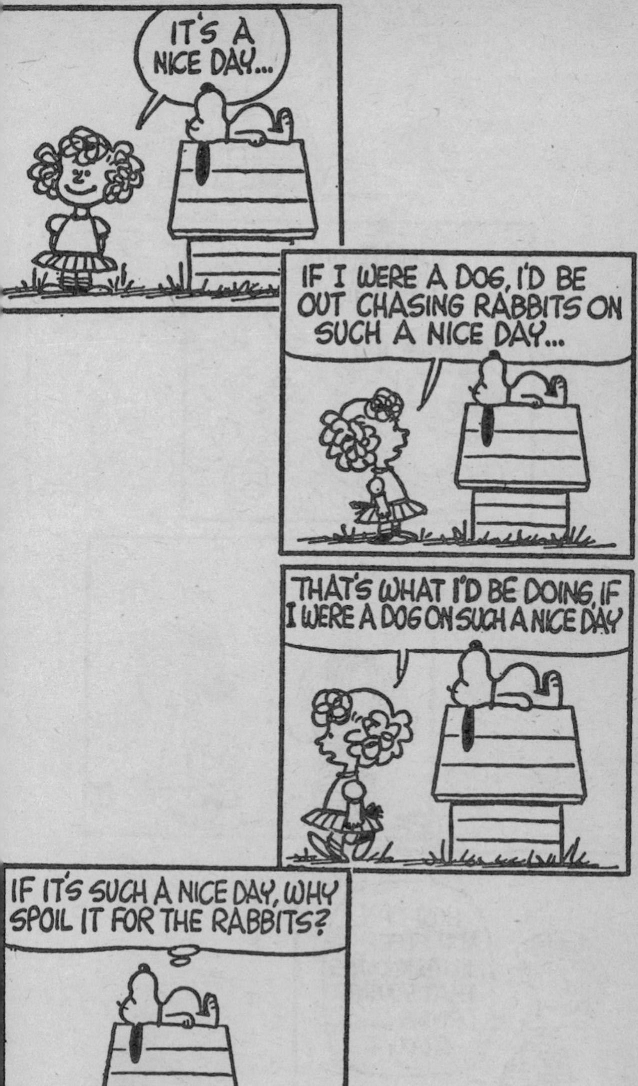
IT'S A NICE DAY...
IF I WERE A DOG, I'D BE OUT CHASING RABBITS ON SUCH A NICE DAY...
THAT'S WHAT I'D BE DOING, IF I WERE A DOG ON SUCH A NICE DAY
IF IT'S SUCH A NICE DAY, WHY SPOIL IT FOR THE RABBITS?

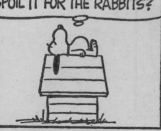

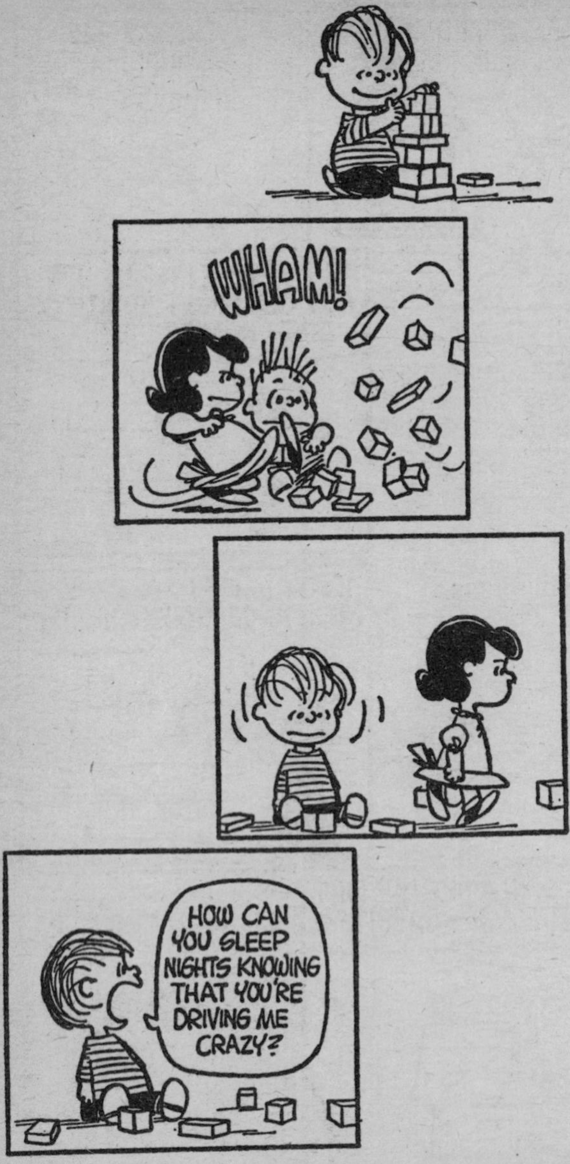
WHAM!
HOW CAN YOU SLEEP NIGHTS KNOWING THAT YOU'RE DRIVING ME CRAZY?

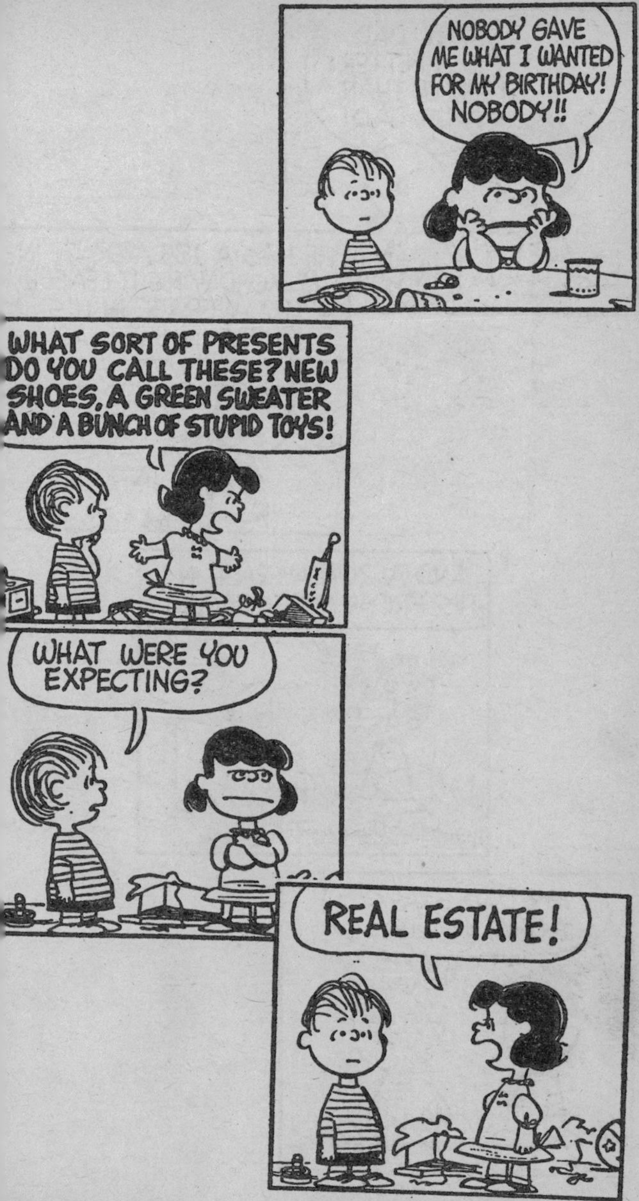
NOBODY GAVE ME WHAT I WANTED FOR MY BIRTHDAY! NOBODY!!
WHAT SORT OF PRESENTS DO YOU CALL THESE? NEW SHOES, A GREEN SWEATER AND A BUNCH OF STUPID TOYS!
WHAT WERE YOU EXPECTING?
REAL ESTATE!

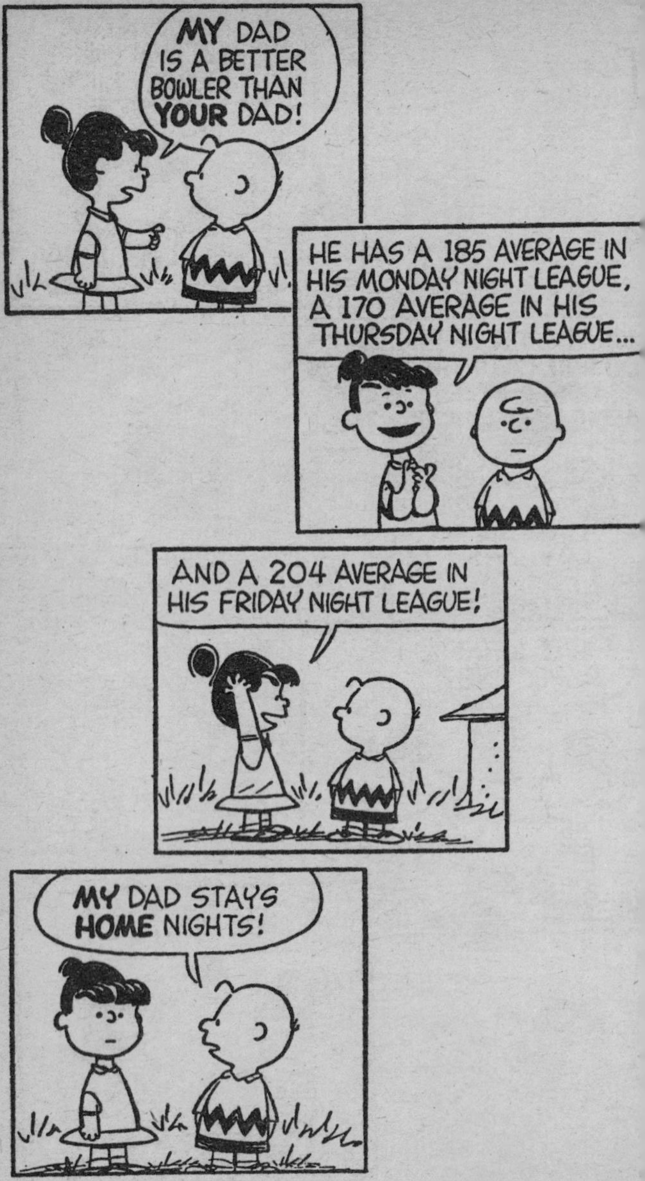
MY DAD IS A BETTER BOWLER THAN YOUR DAD!
HE HAS A 185 AVERAGE IN HIS MONDAY NIGHT LEAGUE, A 170 AVERAGE IN HIS THURSDAY NIGHT LEAGUE...
AND A 204 AVERAGE IN HIS FRIDAY NIGHT LEAGUE!
MY DAD STAYS HOME NIGHTS!

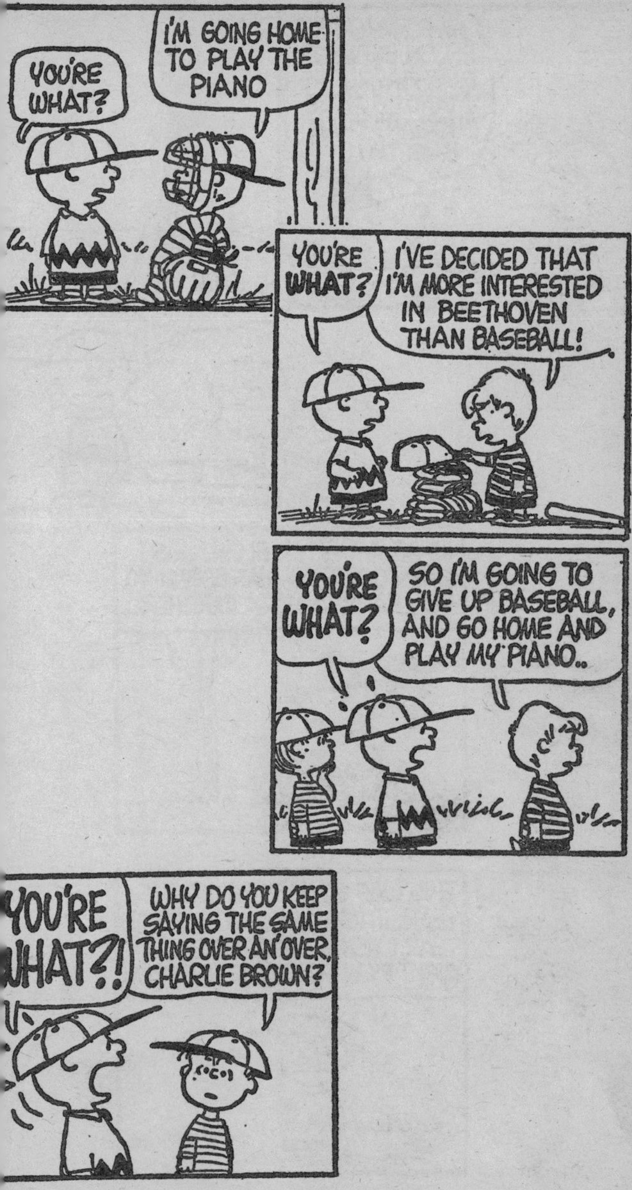

YOU'RE WHAT?
I'M GOING HOME TO PLAY THE PIANO
YOU'RE WHAT?
I'VE DECIDED THAT I'M MORE INTERESTED IN BEETHOVEN THAN BASEBALL!
YOU'RE WHAT?
SO I'M GOING TO GIVE UP BASEBALL, AND GO HOME AND PLAY MY PIANO..
YOU'RE WHAT?!
WHY DO YOU KEEP SAYING THE SAME THING OVER AN' OVER, CHARLIE BROWN?

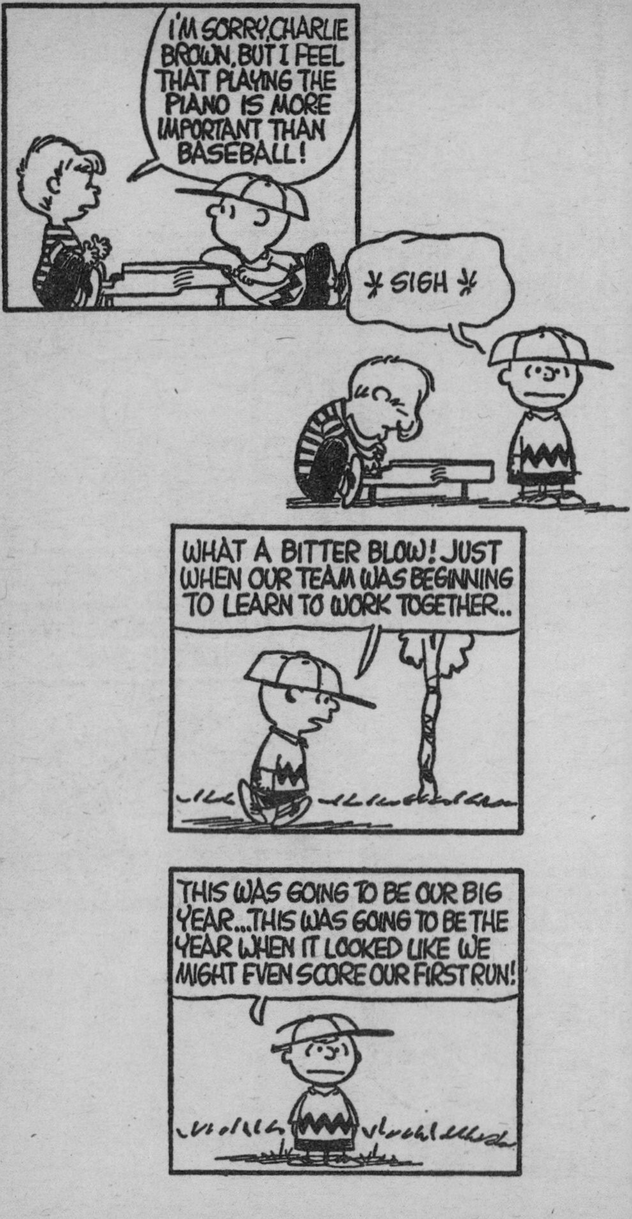
I'M SORRY, CHARLIE BROWN, BUT I FEEL THAT PLAYING THE PIANO IS MORE IMPORTANT THAN BASEBALL!
SIGH
WHAT A BITTER BLOW! JUST WHEN OUR TEAM WAS BEGINNING TO LEARN TO WORK TOGETHER..
THIS WAS GOING TO BE OUR BIG YEAR...THIS WAS GOING TO BE THE YEAR WHEN IT LOOKED LIKE WE MIGHT EVEN SCORE OUR FIRST RUN!

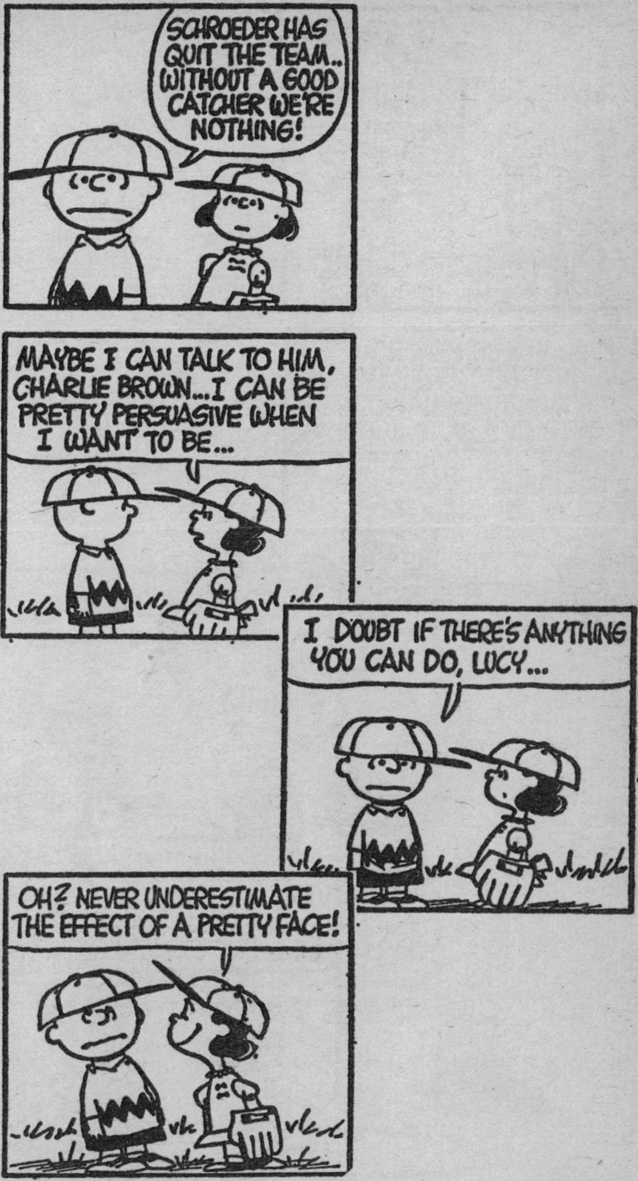
SCHROEDER HAS QUIT THE TEAM.. WITHOUT A GOOD CATCHER WE'RE NOTHING!
MAYBE I CAN TALK TO HIM, CHARLIE BROWN...I CAN BE PRETTY PERSUASIVE WHEN I WANT TO BE...
I DOUBT IF THERE'S ANYTHING YOU CAN DO, LUCY...
OH? NEVER UNDERESTIMATE THE EFFECT OF A PRETTY FACE!

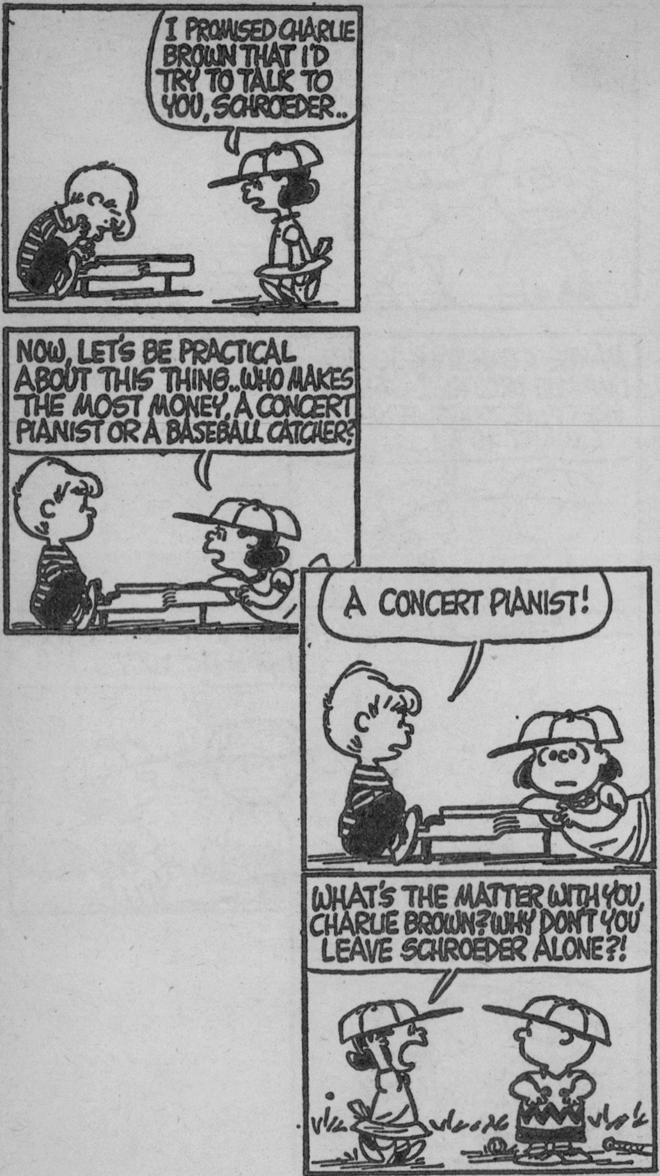
I PROMISED CHARLIE BROWN THAT I'D TRY TO TALK TO YOU, SCHROEDER..
NOW, LET'S BE PRACTICAL ABOUT THIS THING..WHO MAKES THE MOST MONEY, A CONCERT PIANIST OR A BASEBALL CATCHER?
A CONCERT PIANIST!
WHAT'S THE MATTER WITH YOU, CHARLIE BROWN? WHY DON'T YOU LEAVE SCHROEDER ALONE?!

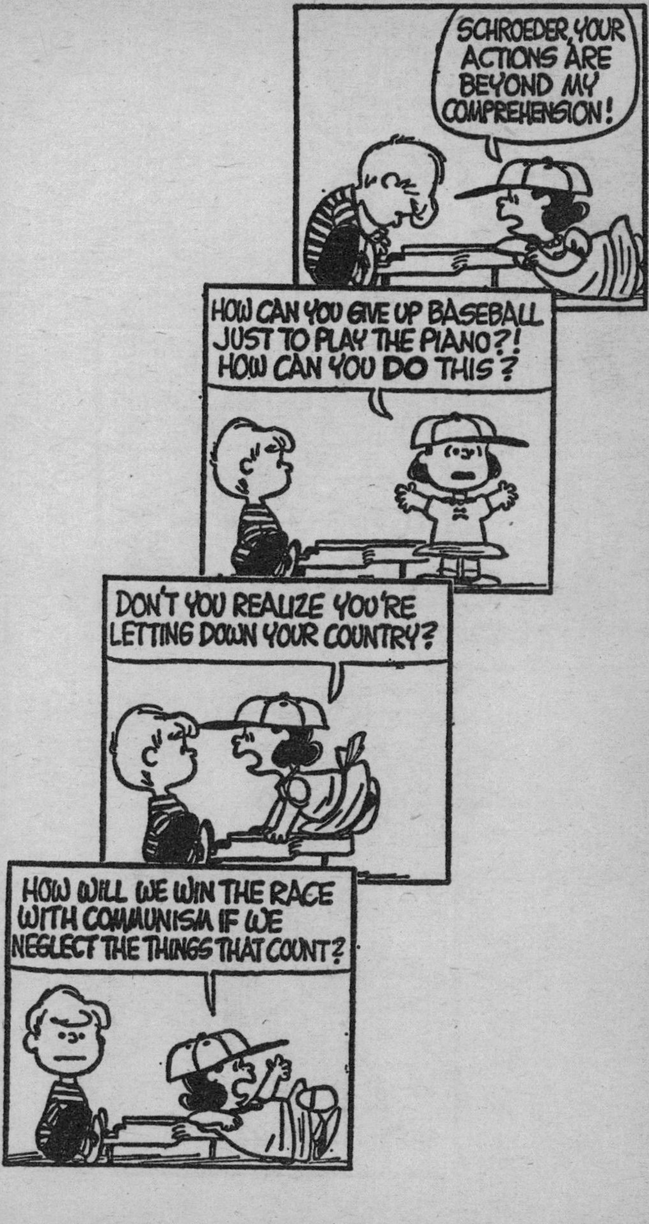
SCHROEDER, YOUR ACTIONS ARE BEYOND MY COMPREHENSION!
HOW CAN YOU GIVE UP BASEBALL JUST TO PLAY THE PIANO?! HOW CAN YOU DO THIS?
DON'T YOU REALIZE YOU'RE LETTING DOWN YOUR COUNTRY?
HOW WILL WE WIN THE RACE WITH COMMUNISM IF WE NEGLECT THE THINGS THAT COUNT?

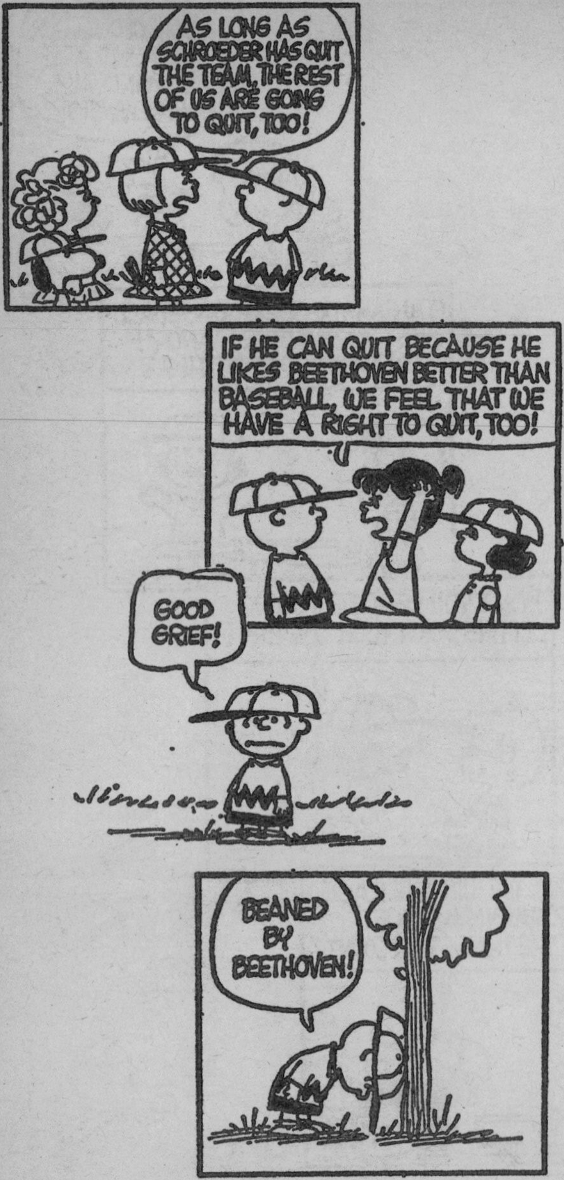
AS LONG AS SCHROEDER HAS QUIT THE TEAM, THE REST OF US ARE GOING TO QUIT, TOO!
IF HE CAN QUIT BECAUSE HE LIKES BEETHOVEN BETTER THAN BASEBALL, WE FEEL THAT WE HAVE A RIGHT TO QUIT, TOO!
GOOD GRIEF!
BEANED BY BEETHOVEN!

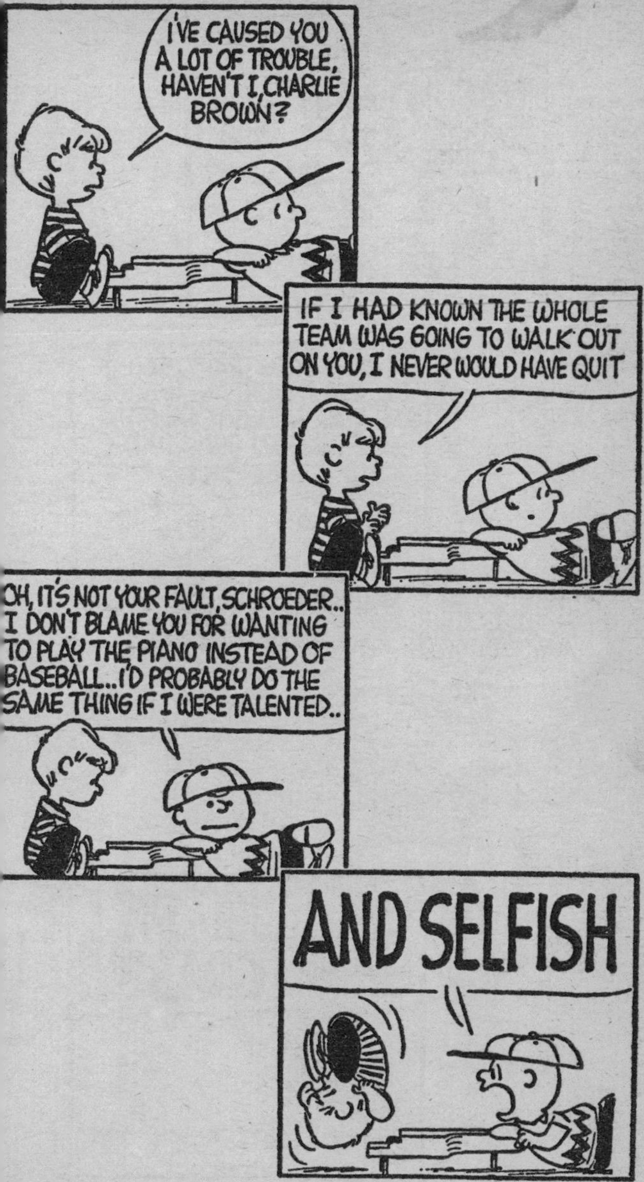
I'VE CAUSED YOU A LOT OF TROUBLE, HAVEN'T I, CHARLIE BROWN?
IF I HAD KNOWN THE WHOLE TEAM WAS GOING TO WALK OUT ON YOU, I NEVER WOULD HAVE QUIT
OH, IT'S NOT YOUR FAULT, SCHROEDER.. I DON'T BLAME YOU FOR WANTING TO PLAY THE PIANO INSTEAD OF BASEBALL..I'D PROBABLY DO THE SAME THING IF I WERE TALENTED..
AND SELFISH

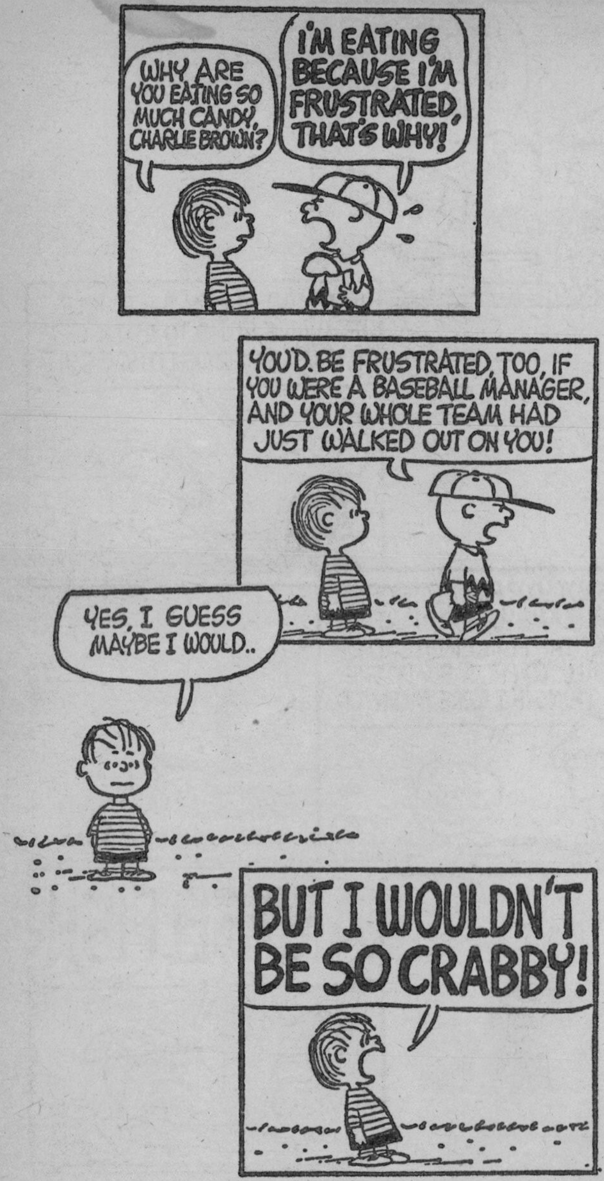
WHY ARE YOU EATING SO MUCH CANDY, CHARLIE BROWN?
I'M EATING BECAUSE I'M FRUSTRATED, THAT'S WHY!
YOU'D BE FRUSTRATED, TOO, IF YOU WERE A BASEBALL MANAGER, AND YOUR WHOLE TEAM HAD JUST WALKED OUT ON YOU!
YES, I GUESS MAYBE I WOULD..
BUT I WOULDN'T BE SO CRABBY!

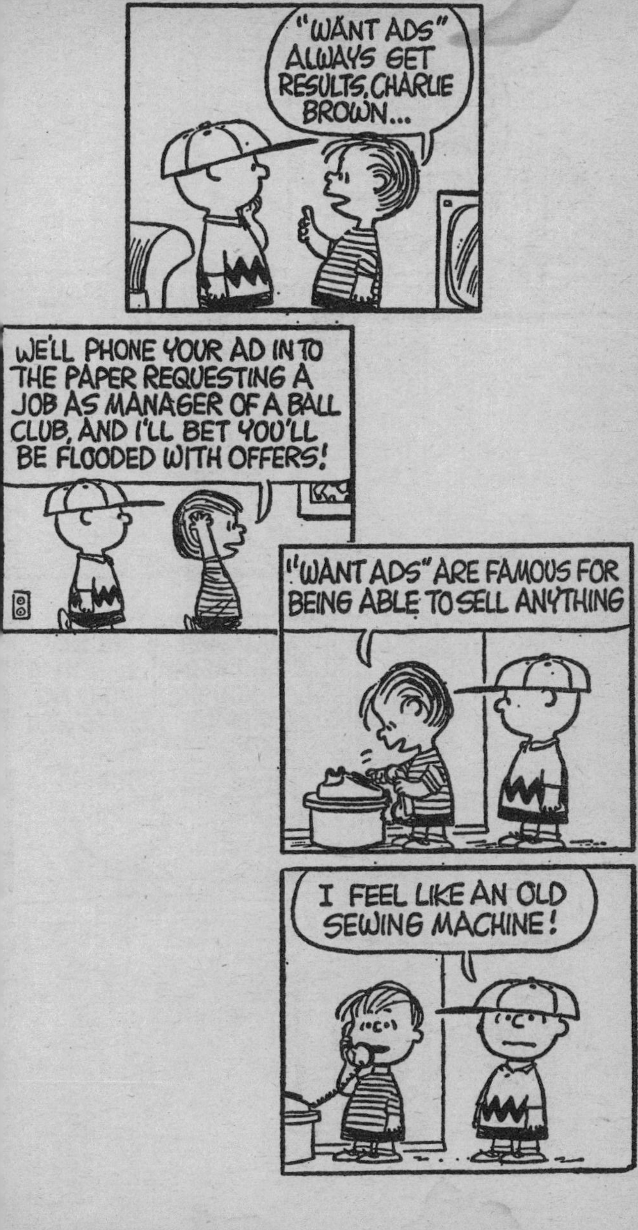
"WANT ADS" ALWAYS GET RESULTS, CHARLIE BROWN...
WE'LL PHONE YOUR AD IN TO THE PAPER REQUESTING A JOB AS MANAGER OF A BALL CLUB, AND I'LL BET YOU'LL BE FLOODED WITH OFFERS!
"WANT ADS" ARE FAMOUS FOR BEING ABLE TO SELL ANYTHING
I FEEL LIKE AN OLD SEWING MACHINE!

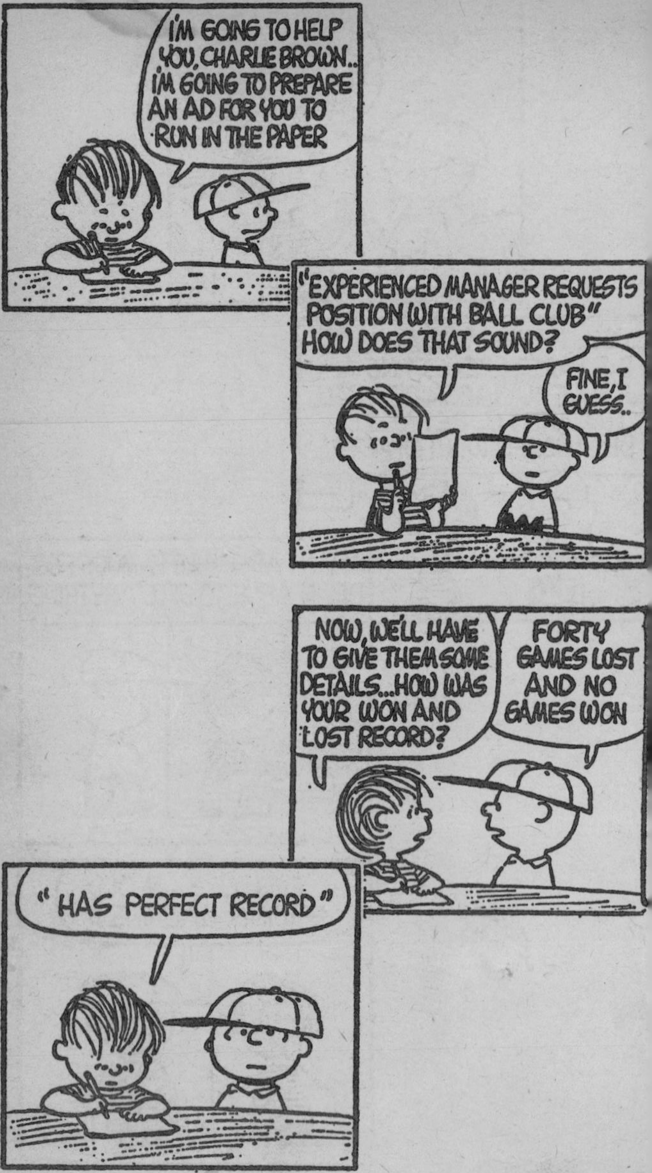
I'M GOING TO HELP YOU, CHARLIE BROWN.. I'M GOING TO PREPARE AN AD FOR YOU TO RUN IN THE PAPER
"EXPERIENCED MANAGER REQUESTS POSITION WITH BALL CLUB" HOW DOES THAT SOUND?
FINE, I GUESS..
NOW, WE'LL HAVE TO GIVE THEM SOME DETAILS...HOW WAS YOUR WON AND LOST RECORD?
FORTY GAMES LOST AND NO GAMES WON
"HAS PERFECT RECORD"